P9-BZE-774

SUPPLY MANAGEMENT FOR VALUE ENHANCEMENT

Lisa M. Ellram
Arizona State University

Thomas Y. Choi
Arizona State University

Published by: Institute for Supply Management, Inc.™
Paul Novak, C.P.M., A.P.P., Chief Executive Officer

© 2000 Institute for Supply Management, Inc.™
P.O. Box 22160 Tempe, AZ 85285-2160 USA
www.ism.ws

INTRODUCTION

Supply management professionals provide many valuable and important contributions to organizations throughout the world, whether they are public, for profit, or non-profit, and across all sectors. The field is quickly evolving and changing, reflecting the evolution of technology, the Internet, heightened professional standards, and increased collaboration between different internal departments, between suppliers, between customers, and between organizations. Supply management is affecting the bottomline more than ever before, and is "value added" for all companies and their financial success.

This new environment, however, requires all supply management professionals to stay on top of the tools, practices, policies, and knowledge relevant not only to supply management, but to the business environment as a whole. ISM is dedicated to building the professional through education and professional development. The ISM Supply Management Knowledge Series (previously known as the NAPM Professional Development Series) was developed to assist the supply management professional do this.

The Series has been updated to include an analysis and discussion of newly emerging trends and the new tools, practices, policies, and knowledge that have developed from these trends. Our goal in publishing the Series is to encourage and support your professional growth and contribute to the image of the profession, and to assist you with learning about and mastering these new skills . . . basically, to help you do your job the best you can.

In addition, the books are a resource for preparing for the C.P.M. and A.P.P. certification exams. The exams were also recently updated and many of the topics addressed in this four-volume series appear on these new exams.

It is my intention that ISM will not only continue its efforts to support and build the supply management profession, but will also add to it. The ISM Supply Management Knowledge Series is a part of these efforts.

Paul Novak, C.P.M., A.P.P.
Chief Executive Officer
ISM
August 2000

ISM – Your Source for Supply Management Resources

Since 1915, the Institute for Supply Management™ (ISM) (formerly the National Association of Purchasing Management (NAPM)), has served thousands of supply management professionals from around the world. Domestically, ISM works with affiliated associations across the country to continually keep its members well informed, and trained on the latest trends and developments in the field.

The information available from ISM is extensive. One of the greatest resources is the ISM Web site, www.ism.ws. In addition to general information, this expansive site features a vast database of supply management information, much of which is available solely to members. Information includes a listing of general supply management references as well as an extensive article database, listings of products and seminars available, a periodicals listing, an Online Career Center with job listings and resumes posted, contact information for ISM affiliate organizations nationwide, and links to other related Web sites.

The monthly Manufacturing and Non-Manufacturing ISM *Report On Business*®, including the PMI in the manufacturing survey, continues to be one of the key economic indicators available today. ISM members receive this valuable report in the pages of *Inside Supply Management*™ magazine, one of the many benefits of membership.

ISM also publishes *The Journal of Supply Chain Management*, a one-of-a-kind publication designed especially for experienced supply management professionals. Authored exclusively by accomplished practitioners and academicians, this quarterly publication targets purchasing and supply management issues, leading-edge research, long-term strategic developments, emerging trends, and more.

Members also enjoy discounts on a wide variety of educational products and services, along with reduced enrollment fees, for educational seminars and conferences held throughout the country each year. Topics cover the entire supply management spectrum.

For executives interested in professional certification, ISM administers the Certified Purchasing Manager (C.P.M.) and Accredited Purchasing Practitioner (A.P.P.) programs. Members receive discounts on test preparation/study materials and C.P.M./A.P.P. exam fees.

To provide a forum for educational enhancement and networking, ISM holds the Annual International Supply Management Conference. This is a unique opportunity for members and non-members alike to learn from each other and share success strategies.

To learn more about ISM and the many ways it can help you advance your career, or to join online, visit ISM on the Web at www.ism.ws. To apply for membership by telephone, please call ISM customer service at 800/888-6276 or 480/752-6276, extension 401.

The ISM Supply Management Knowledge Series

Volume 1
The Supply Management Process
Alan R. Raedels

Volume 2
The Supply Management Environment
Stanley E. Fawcett

Volume 3
Supply Management for Value Enhancement
Lisa M. Ellram and Thomas Y. Choi

Volume 4
The Supply Management Leadership Process
Anna Flynn and Sam Farney

SERIES OVERVIEW

In the past decade, purchasing has moved to the center stage of the organization as it has become increasingly clear that purchasing and supply management can make a significant contribution to organizational success. Beyond simply reducing prices for purchased goods and services, purchasing can add value to organizations in many ways, including supporting organizational strategy, improving inventory management, forging closer working relationships with key suppliers, and maintaining an active awareness of supply market trends. The ability of purchasing to significantly contribute to organizational success is the core of this four-book series.

While differences exist among various types of organizations, industries, business sectors, regions of the world, and types of items purchased, these books provide an overview of current issues in purchasing and supply management. The topics covered in this series range from the basics of good purchasing practice to leading-edge, value enhancement strategies. These four books provide an excellent survey of the core principles and practices common to all sectors within the field of purchasing and supply management.

These four volumes were designed to support the Institute for Supply Management™ (ISM) (formerly the National Association of Purchasing Management (NAPM)) certification program leading to the Accredited Purchasing Practitioner (A.P.P.) and Certified Purchasing Manager (C.P.M.) designations. They also provide practical and current coverage of key topics in the field for those interested in enhancing their knowledge. They also can serve as useful textbooks for college courses in purchasing.

The textbooks are organized around the four modules of the C.P.M. exam as follows:

1. *The Supply Management Process* (for C.P.M.s and A.P.P.s)
2. *The Supply Management Environment* (for C.P.M.s and A.P.P.s)
3. *Supply Management for Value Enhancement Strategies* (for C.P.M.s only)
4. *The Supply Management Leadership Process* (for C.P.M.s only)

Volume 1, *The Supply Management Process*, focuses on the overall purchasing process and its major elements. It looks at the requisitioning process, sourcing, bidding, and supplier evaluation, and offers an overview of cost and contract management. This volume also examines how technology has changed procurement techniques and provides a summary of the key legal issues facing purchasers.

Volume 2, *The Supply Management Environment*, explores how the ever-changing environment in which purchasers operate is affecting their roles today and in the future. Volume 2 provides an overview of purchasing's role in strategy and looks at how globalization and just-in-time/mass customization are affecting purchasing. This volume also explores issues related to negotiations, quality, reengineering, and supply chain management. It examines the increased role and impact of information technology on purchasing, and looks at what skill sets will be required for success in purchasing in the future.

Volume 3, *Supply Management for Value Enhancement Strategies*, explores a number of traditional and leading-edge approaches for increasing purchasing's contributions to organizational success. The volume begins by looking at outsourcing and lease versus buy issues. It then delves into the many issues associated with inventory management, including inventory classification and disposal. Specific value enhancement methods, such as standardization, value analysis, early supplier involvement, and target costing, are also presented. The volume closes with a discussion of developing and using forecast data, and offers an overview of specific strategies to apply in various purchasing situations.

Volume 4, *The Supply Management Leadership Process*, provides an overview of key general management issues specifically applied to purchasing activities and purchasing's role in the organization. It begins with an overview of strategic planning and budgeting processes, and continues by presenting specific issues related to effectively recruiting, managing, and retaining good employees. Volume 4 then discusses the role of operating policies and procedures, tools to manage workflow, and performance monitoring. It ends with a presentation of how to most effectively present purchasing performance results within the organization.

It has been a privilege to edit this series for ISM and to work with an excellent group of authors. The authors' practical and theoretical knowledge has contributed to the quality of these books. I hope you find them both useful and interesting.

Lisa M. Ellram
Series Editor

PREFACE

Supply Management for Value Enhancement Strategies, like the other three in this series, is based on the newly revised ninth edition of the *C.P.M. Study Guide*. The *Study Guide* is intended to assist those preparing for the Certified Purchasing Manager (C.P.M.) Examination. This book is also intended to provide an overview of best practices in purchasing and value enhancement activities to support the ongoing improvement efforts of purchasing and supply management practitioners. The *C.P.M. Study Guide* and its predecessors are the result of the collective effort of a large number of purchasing practitioners and academics who acted as editors, authors, and reviewers. We would like to thank all of them for their fine work. In particular, we would like to thank Alan Raedels, who took on the primary task of editor for the 2000 edition of the *C.P.M. Study Guide*.

We would also like to thank Cynthia Zigmund, who supplied technical editorial guidance, and Scott Sturzl, who provided content-based editorial guidance. Their timely and helpful feedback improved the quality of this publication.

Any inaccuracies or omissions are solely the responsibility of the authors.

Lisa M. Ellram
Thomas Y. Choi

To the many wonderful women who have given me love and support: my mother, Aime Ellram; sisters, Ruth Lubansky and Heidi Ellram; my friend, Sue Siferd; my cat Venus; and my writers group, Ginger Hutton, Susan Price, and Ann Wright-Edwards, who support me no matter what I write. Many thanks and blessings to all the others too numerous to mention.

Lisa M. Ellram

To my mentors, Dr. Jeffrey Liker and Dr. Chan Hahn, for teaching me over the years and for opening the door to the world of purchasing and supply management.

Thomas Y. Choi

CONTENTS

Chapter 1: The Value Enhancement Concept

Chapter 2: Lease Versus Buy Analysis and Other Leveraging Tools

Chapter 3: Inventory Control and Managerial Issues

Chapter 4: Inventory Strategies and Disposal

Chapter 5: Value Enhancement Programs

Chapter 6: The Role of Purchasing and Supply in New Product Development

Chapter 7: Planning and Developing Sourcing Strategy Based on Forecast Data

Chapter 8: Purchasing Information and Strategy Development

CHAPTER 1

THE VALUE ENHANCEMENT CONCEPT

How can purchasing and supply management (PSM) contribute to organizational success through supporting outsourcing and privatization efforts?

Chapter Objectives

- To introduce the concept of value enhancement and purchasing's role in value enhancement
- To develop an understanding of the strategic importance of outsourcing to long-term organizational success
- To provide a framework for assessing a potential outsourcing (make or buy) decision
- To develop an understanding of privatization and its similarity to outsourcing
- To define the role and contribution of purchasing and supply management to the outsourcing process

What is Value Enhancement?

Value enhancement is a critical concept for purchasing and supply management. While organizations have long looked to purchasing and supply management as a source of cost reduction, value enhancement goes beyond simple cost reduction. Value enhancement is an approach that looks at how to get more worth for an organization's spending. The focus is not simply on reducing cost, but reducing cost while ensuring that all of the organization's quality and

1

delivery needs are met, or holding costs at the same level while improving other performance parameters.

Why PSM Should Care about Value Enhancement

In most situations, it is possible to get a lower price for the organization's purchases of goods and services. However, a lower price may mean lower quality, less reliable delivery, less supplier responsiveness, or a host of other negatives if the buyer does not focus simultaneously on price and value. Focusing only on price is a reactive approach — doing what it takes to meet price objectives without regard to the impact on the rest of the organization. Such a focus undermines the performance of other functions and the organization as a whole. A low-price, low-quality supplier may contribute to higher inventory costs, because extra inventory must be held to ensure that an adequate supply of good-quality items is available when needed. In the case of a service, a low-quality supplier may have to bill more hours in order to get the job right, thereby eliminating the impact of any savings in the hourly rate. A low-quality supplier may also create extra paperwork costs as a result of tracking quality problems, may cause goods or services to arrive late to customers, as well as a host of similar problems.

Consequently, a key element of the value enhancement philosophy is to view all purchasing decisions from a holistic, big-picture perspective. A holistic perspective recognizes that in optimizing each activity within an organization, the overall results may be suboptimized. By not considering the interactions and potential synergy among activities and processes (for example, using suppliers that are quality-certified can reduce inventory and cycle time), the overall performance of the organization may be diminished as each area pursues its own goals in isolation. Thus, the issue of how and what to buy from whom at what price has important implications throughout an organization. The professional purchaser considers the broader implications of supplier selection, supplier management, and cost management on the long-term performance of his or her organization. As such, a value enhancement approach serves multiple objectives in delivering benefits to an organization. Proactive purchasers take this approach to increase their visibility and contributions to the organization.

Organization of This Book

The first volume in this series, *The Purchasing Process*,[1] highlights the importance of using tools such as price and cost analysis to contribute to the organization's bottomline. This book considers other approaches, including the proper use of outsourcing; lease versus buy analysis; inventory management and disposal issues; specific value enhancement programs, such as value analysis and standardization; early purchasing and supplier involvement in new product and service development; and forecasting, developing, and using market knowledge. This chapter begins by focusing on outsourcing, an increasingly important decision in supply chain design and purchasing strategy.

Critical Issues in Outsourcing/Privatization

According to Charles Fine, in his recent book, *Clockspeed*,[2] what to outsource (make versus buy) is the most critical decision that an organization faces. In fact, according to Fine, knowing what and how to outsource is the ultimate core competency that an organization can have in these rapidly changing times. Yet many organizations do not do a good job of analyzing the outsourcing decision, and consequently, they end up insourcing — bringing outsourced activities back into the organization. Outsourcing is also referred to as the *make or buy decision*. The decision to outsource involves analyzing whether the organization should make an item in-house or buy it from a supplier. An organization also must decide whether to have required services, such as janitorial and security services, performed by its employees or by an outside contractor.

Outsourcing can be a value-enhancing activity. By outsourcing manufacturing services and processes that are not strategic in nature, the organization can focus its attention on the issues that are most important to customers and the activities that the organization needs to perform best. The top reasons identified for outsourcing are:

1. Improve organizational focus
2. Access world-class capabilities
3. Reduce and control operating costs
4. Use resources not available internally

5. Free resources for other purposes
6. Accelerate engineering benefits
7. Function is difficult to manage/out of control
8. Make capital funds available
9. Obtain a cash infusion
10. Share risks[3]

Strategic Importance of Outsourcing

As mentioned by Fine[4] and others,[5][6] an organization must take care not to outsource its critical competitive capabilities. Thus, the first step in outsourcing is to determine what the organization's key success factors are. By outsourcing things that the organization does well, and that are critical to its success, it may experience diminished performance, thereby reducing its competitive position. As part of the make or buy decision, organizations should carefully consider whether the item being considered for outsourcing is:

- Important to its market dominance
- Difficult to imitate
- Based on unique knowledge, experience, or resources that the organization possesses
- Clearly superior to that of the competition

If the organization answers yes to any of these questions for a particular item, outsourcing is likely to reduce the organization's competitive posture and is not advisable.

Today, in this time of rapidly changing technology and market dominance, it is also important to look ahead when outsourcing. Is the item or service under consideration for outsourcing likely to increase in importance? Could outsourcing hurt the organization's probability of success in the future? Figure 1.1 shows the decision-making process an organization should follow in screening its outsourcing ideas for strategic impact.

FIGURE 1.1
Make or Buy Decision-making Process

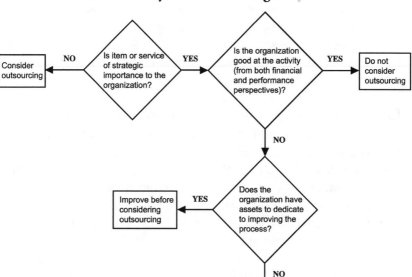

One visible example of outsourcing is in the automotive industry. Many automobile firms outsourced myriad processes during the 1980s. This continued into the late 1990s with General Motor's spin-off of Delphi, its formerly captive auto parts supplier. Today, auto makers are outsourcing entire subassemblies and subsystems to suppliers. Rather than buying individual parts, such as wiper blades to use in manufacturing, many auto makers have the supplier serve more in the capacity of a subcontractor, by providing the complete wiper assembly, including the wiper motor. Yet not everything in the automotive industry is being outsourced. For example, Honda of America Manufacturing is well known for its engine expertise in the automotive, motorcycle, lawnmower, and small-generator markets. It would be a foolish business decision for Honda to outsource the manufacturing of its engines.

Other Considerations in Outsourcing

As indicated earlier in this chapter, a strategic assessment should be performed before entertaining any outsourcing decisions. A number of other factors are also relevant, including the long-term supply implications of outsourcing, labor and other organizational constraints, a supplier's scalability, quality considerations, risk, a supplier's support capability, socioeconomic goals and objectives, and an organization's expertise in the area under consideration for outsourcing. Each of these issues is presented in the following paragraphs.

Long-term supply implications – This represents one type of potential risk. Once an organization has divested itself of the ability to manufacture an item or provide a service internally, it may be difficult, costly, and time-consuming to bring that item back in-house. For example, a major manufacturer of chemicals and polymers, which prefers to remain anonymous, has outsourced all of its logistics operations, from transportation to warehousing/distribution and order processing. It sold or otherwise divested itself of all physical assets associated with logistics operations: tractors and trailers, buildings, forklifts, and so on. Yet, due to the scale and complexity of its operations, the manufacturer finds that it is still involved in the day-to-day management of logistics activities and has extensive internal logistics staff. The savings it has enjoyed has been primarily in hourly labor. Had it known in advance that the management requirements would be so great, the manufacturer might not have decided to outsource. However, at this point, it would be cost-prohibitive to reverse the decision. The manufacturer is now committed to outsourcing.

Such a commitment can be even more serious if the item or service being outsourced is given to a single supplier, and that supplier has special expertise, tooling, or equipment to provide that item. The organization thus has little freedom in source selection and can develop an unhealthy dependency on a supplier. The supplier may take advantage of that dependence by raising prices or reducing service levels or quality if the buying organization has no alternatives. The supplier may become complacent in its technology and innovation efforts, which puts the buying organization at a competitive disadvantage. In some cases, however, the fixed investment required to have two or more capable sources may render outsourcing an unattractive decision. Such possibilities should be considered as part of the outsourcing decision process.

Labor and other organizational constraints – These may also be factors. The availability of a stable and trained work force, particularly if the organization has good relations with the work force, is an important consideration in the make or buy analysis. For example, Case Corporation, a manufacturer, designer, and distributor of agricultural equipment, has an excellent, highly skilled work force. It has outsourced generic processes, such as machining and fabrication, while retaining the manufacturing of critical components. Still, if business is down, Case will bring some of its outsourced volume back in-house to use its work force and avoid layoffs. Thus, outsourcing has provided Case the flexibility to better manage its work force.[7]

Frequently, organizations view outsourcing as a way to reduce their labor costs. They may have a mature or unionized work force that is well paid, with excellent benefits. They decide that they could save money by outsourcing to a company that pays lower wages and provides fewer benefits. Organizations need to remember that they often get what they pay for. A poorly paid labor force may have lower skills and higher turnover and absenteeism, thereby creating unreliability and the constant need for retraining, which potentially increases the cost of doing business. As in all purchases, a low price does not necessarily yield low costs.

The supplier's scalability – The supplier's scalability is another concern in outsourcing. As mentioned previously, Case uses outsourcing to buffer its own labor force, allowing the outside supplier's volume to fluctuate rather than absorbing it internally. But what if the outside supplier depends on Case for volume and has to lay off some of its work force as a result? This, in turn, will result in increased training and hiring costs for the supplier, which Case must ultimately bear in the price it pays to the supplier.

It is risky to be a very large customer to a supplier, because small fluctuations in the buying organization's volume may be amplified at the supplier level. Similarly, a small supplier may not be able to absorb volume upswings as readily. Thus, it is important to consider the projected direction and magnitude of the buying organization's volume in selecting a supplier. Can the supplier grow with the organization?

Quality considerations – These considerations are extremely important in outsourcing. Whether the organization outsources or provides a service or manufactures an item internally should be invisible to the internal customer. Historically, many organizations have found it easier to "do it themselves" when the quality requirements for a particular product or service were extremely tight and close control was required. However, this is no longer true. Because suppliers are experts in what they do, many suppliers compete on the basis of meeting strict specifications for individual customers. Quality concerns make a thorough audit of the supplier's quality systems and processes essential in any outsourcing decision. The buying organization must not only consider the quality of the item the supplier is providing, but also the quality of all of the relevant interfaces, such as delivery, accurate invoices, good customer service, and so on.

Risk – Risk may exist in a number of ways when a company is analyzing the make or buy decision. A company that chooses to make a product must face the hazards of business and changing economic conditions, factors over which it has little control. Such factors include cyclical and long-term trends in the product's industry, changes in demand, technological advances, and unpredictable factors, such as government regulations, tax policies, and international conflicts. These are all risks present in the external environment.

Another risk involves miscalculating the future strategic importance of an item that is outsourced. The impact of such a decision is extremely hard to predict and, perhaps, even more difficult to reverse. A classic case of this was IBM's decision to outsource personal computer (PC) parts. It chose to outsource the microprocessor to Intel and the operating system to Microsoft. Intel and Microsoft have thrived in the PC business, and they are considered two of the most successful computer companies in the world. IBM, while highly successful in other arenas, lost about $2 billion in its PC business in 1998.[8]

Specific risks occur when an organization becomes dependent on a supplier. The supplier may then behave opportunistically, putting the buying organization in a "hostage" situation. Opportunism by the supplier is more likely in situations where the supplier has unique assets that the buying organization depends on. These could be equipment and tooling, information systems, or specific knowledge. It is also more likely in volatile environments, in which the supplier can take advantage of shortages.[9] It is, therefore, important to set up a situation where competition is possible or where there is mutual dependence between the buyer and the seller in order to avoid the risk of opportunism.

A risk also includes the loss of skills and knowledge that can happen in some outsourcing situations. For example, Kodak outsourced all of its information technology to IBM in 1990. Does Kodak still have the expertise to "take it back" in-house if it deems that IBM can no longer perform up to its standards? It seems that it would be costly and time-consuming to reverse that decision.

Supplier support capability – Supplier support capability must also be considered when outsourcing. For technical items, a supplier should be able to provide support and stand behind its products. If the supplier does not have this capability, it can be a burden for the buying organization to attempt to locate a third party that is capable. On the other hand, a buying firm may not have the expertise to make or acquire certain critical components of a product that it seeks to produce. In such circumstances, buying the component from current or potential suppliers is advantageous. This is true in the automotive industry, where the electronics have become increasingly complex. In many cases, auto makers are buying a "black box," and they depend on the supplier's technical capability.

Socioeconomic goals and objectives – These goals and objectives are also a consideration in outsourcing. There has been some concern that small and minority suppliers are being shut out by increased outsourcing. Outsourcing often involves full-service suppliers, and many small and minority firms are smaller, niche providers.

Level of expertise – The level of expertise in the area to be outsourced should also be considered. If the buying organization has a high level of expertise in the area, outsourcing the item may create a loss of that expertise. The following question must be addressed: Is that expertise important to the organization's success? For example, Eastman Kodak has an award-winning cafeteria in its headquarters. Nonetheless, it decided to outsource the cafeteria because it was so far removed from the nature of its other business that it was a burden to manage. The party that took over the cafeteria has done an excellent job, with no impact on Kodak's competitive success.[10]

How to Conduct a Make or Buy/Outsourcing Analysis

Today, many activities are candidates for outsourcing, such as information technology, facilities management, and organization fleets. Organizations are increasingly turning over their office supplies, parts, and tools operations to "integrated suppliers" that manage the purchasing, inventory management, and disbursement of such items to the organization's personnel. Before undertaking a make or buy analysis, the organization should do a strategic assessment of the item under consideration, as detailed in Figure 1.1. The organization should also review the factors presented in the "Other Considerations in Outsourcing" section of this chapter as it conducts the outsourcing analysis.

Determination of Feasibility

The feasibility stage begins after the strategic assessment has determined that this purchase is a good candidate for insourcing or outsourcing. If the organization is considering producing an item that it currently buys, it must evaluate whether it is feasible to make the product or provide the service. Does it have, or can it acquire, the necessary production equipment, personnel, material, space, supervision, overhead, maintenance, taxes, insurance, and associated items? If the answer is no, it should continue to buy the item. On the other hand, if it is considering outsourcing, the organization must assess the supply market capabilities. Are there sources available? Do the potential sources meet capacity, quality, and other organizational needs? Are they interested? If the answer to any of these key questions is no, the buying organization must consider whether it wants to develop a supplier to meet its needs. Supplier development can be a costly and time-consuming process, which is presented in the second volume of this series.

Determination of Need

Determination of need involves considering the volume and the timing of the requirements, as well as considering whether a complete outsourcing/insourcing solution is needed. This involves noting what aspects of the purchase are strategic and where the organization has expertise versus the supply market. For example, when Nynex (now Bell Atlantic) was deciding to outsource construction management, it considered simply hiring a general contractor to manage the entire process. It also segmented the purchase into three parts: construction management, professional services, and zone general contractor. Bell Atlantic/Nynex found that by separating these segments, it allowed each part to focus on what it was good at, and Bell Atlantic/Nynex could focus on what it was good at — managing the contracts. It achieved better performance and lower total cost of ownership by retaining more of the management than originally anticipated.[11]

Total Cost of Ownership Analysis

Performing a total cost of ownership analysis is an important approach to understanding the impact of an insourcing or outsourcing decision on the organization's costs. This concept is presented more fully in the first volume of this series. The basic approach is to determine the total of all costs to the organization if it makes the item or purchases the item. To answer this question, the incremental costs for that individual firm must be analyzed and compared. Such an assessment must include an analysis of all major cost components, a sensitivity analysis, and a break-even analysis.

Analysis of all cost components – This includes the direct costs of materials, labor, energy, overhead, transportation, inventory, quality, obsolescence, and capital costs. In outsourcing, organizations often overlook the fact that they may have to retain employees to

Supply Management for Value Enhancement

manage outsourced relationships. Another common mistake is to recognize savings in wages, when only parts of jobs will be eliminated and no wages will be saved.

Sensitivity analysis – Sensitivity analysis should also be performed. This "what-if" analysis takes into account that many of the costs used in modeling the outsourcing decision are estimates. For example, an organization might assume that it will need to retain three of 30 employees to manage the outsourced process. What if that estimate is wrong? What if six internal employees are needed? A sensitivity analysis should be performed for all assumptions in which there is some degree of uncertainty. Costs of make versus buy should be calculated for the best, worst, and expected scenarios. In cases where some assumptions are very sensitive, in that a small change in the estimate would change the decision from make to buy or vice versa, special care needs to be taken to get the best information possible. It is worth investing time and effort into gaining more certainty for those items.

Break-even analysis – Break-even analysis can be used to show at what volumes one alternative, such as insourcing, might be more economical than outsourcing. Break-even analysis also shows at what volume of production the organization will stop incurring losses and begin to produce profits from an activity. This concept is also presented in some depth in the first book of this series. Break-even analysis can be used in conjunction with sensitivity analysis to show at what point make is preferred to buy, or vice versa. Figure 1.2 illustrates the use of a break-even analysis to examine the sensitivity of volume in the outsourcing decision. This figure shows that at 23 million forms or $500,000, the organization is indifferent to make or buy from a financial perspective. If the volume exceeds 23 million forms, printing the forms internally is preferred from strictly a financial perspective. Many other factors, such as distraction from primary competency, should also be weighed in making this decision. The make or buy decision can have a long-term, strategic impact that is difficult to reverse.

FIGURE 1.2
Sample Break-even Analysis Chart

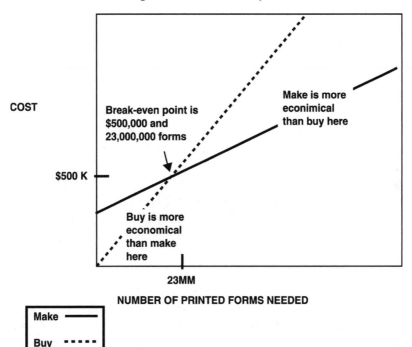

COST

Break-even point is
$500,000 and
23,000,000 forms

Make is more
econimical
than buy here

$500 K

Buy is more
economical
than make
here

23MM

NUMBER OF PRINTED FORMS NEEDED

Make ——

Buy -----

Example of Total Cost of Ownership Analysis Applied to a Make or Buy Decision

An increasingly common decision that organizations face today is whether they should manage their own parts inventory and ordering for small-dollar, high-variety parts, components, and supplies. A manufacturer of custom medical testing equipment faced this decision. Its small-dollar maintenance, repair, and operating supplies; nuts and bolts; and packaging were overwhelming in variety. The organization had about 600 suppliers for approximately 10,000 items in this class of products alone. Inventories and obsolescence were high, the paperwork was overwhelming, efficiencies were low, and shortages were commonplace. The organization knew it needed to change its processes. It looked into integrated supply — having one or a handful of multiline distributors handle all of these items, rather than ordering from a huge number of manufacturers and small distributors. In investigating this possibility, the firm decided to simultaneously change its process so that these multiline distributors would handle all of the inventory management, order placement, and putaway, and provide one monthly bill: integrated supply.

Because the organization was purchasing such a broad array of items and many of its current distributors had exclusive distribution territories, the multiline distributors had to buy from other distributors, thereby increasing the markup. Thus, some of the prices paid would actually go up. Rather than making a simple price-to-price comparison, the organization did a total cost of ownership analysis. The new prices that it would pay would be landed prices, which included freight. In addition, its inventories and obsolescence would go down, because the suppliers would manage the inventory better than the organization had. In addition, some jobs could be eliminated because the supplier was going to place all the orders, monitor inventory, put inventory away, and provide one monthly bill. Previously, the organization had received hundreds of shipments and hundreds of invoices each month. Figure 1.3 shows a comparison of the make (perform internally) or buy (use integrated supply). On a price-to-price comparison, outsourcing was 4 percent higher. But on a total cost comparison, it was 4.7 percent lower. An unexpected benefit of outsourcing was that the organization had chosen integrated suppliers that were experts. As these experts spent time at the manufacturing site and saw how inventory was used, they came up with suggestions for standardizing, substituting, and generally lowering costs. By the second year, costs had come down another 4 percent, so that the total cost of the outsourced alternative was now about the same as the original price of doing it internally, but in addition the organization enjoyed tremendous savings in overhead.[12]

Post-Audit Evaluation of Make or Buy Decision

Organizations increasingly use post-audits of make or buy decisions to determine if they realized the expected results or financial returns. Such an analysis may point out that critical costs were missed in the initial analysis or that unanticipated savings were enjoyed, as described in the integrated supply example in the previous section. The post-audit is an important process in learning how make or buy decisions have been made and how they can be improved in the future. The post-audit process may result in no change in processes, a fine-tuning of the details of the decision, or a reversal of the decision (bringing the item back in-house or finding a new supplier).

Figure 1.3
Use of Total Cost of Ownership Analysis to
Support an Outsourcing Decision

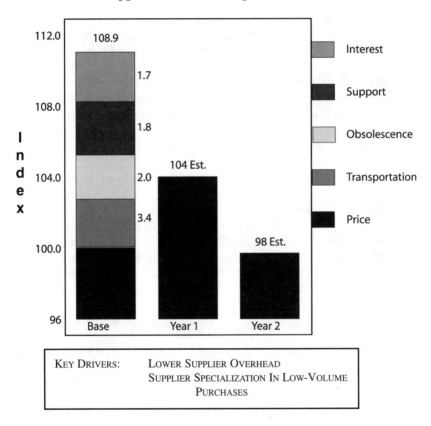

The team considered total cost when justifying the program. Although the material price index rose by approximately 4 percent, the organization saved in the areas of support, interest, obsolescence, and transportation. Further savings are now being realized as the suppliers consolidate their supply bases and apply their expertise to component selection, standardization, and simplification.

Privatization/Outsourcing

Privatization transfers the delivery and/or performance of a public service from employees of the government to private contractors (for example, a municipality hires a sanitation contractor rather than maintaining its own sanitation department). Privatization also refers to the transfer of government-owned enterprises to private investors. Like outsourcing, privatization is a version of a make or buy decision, whereby organizations buy functions that previously were part of their own responsibilities. As organizations downsize and examine the value added by internal functions, many functions are being outsourced. Examples include motor pools, graphics, and cafeteria operations.

Applicability of Privatization

Because more than 80,000 government entities exist in the United States (one federal, 50 state, and the remainder local), privatization is widely applicable to the public sector. Competition provided by the private sector can be healthy, and it often makes government agencies more responsive. Privatization is a worldwide trend that has been pursued vigorously in the international arena.

Issues in Privatization

The issues to be explored in privatization are similar to the issues explored concerning outsourcing. Some of the key questions to consider are listed in Table 1.1. Because most of the issues and decision-making criteria that apply to outsourcing also apply to privatization, they will not be repeated here. This section will focus on the issues that are unique to privatization.

TABLE 1.1
Important Questions to Consider in Privatizing or Outsourcing

1.	Is the process or function part of the organization's core capabilities?
2.	Are capable suppliers available in the market today?
3.	What type of supplier relationship is needed?
4.	What will be the impact on direct and indirect costs?
5.	What will be the impact on service levels?
6.	What is the current level of integration with other parts of the organization?
7.	What type of delivery, quality, capacity, price, and service level must the supplier provide?
8.	Are there any intellectual property issues that need to be considered?
9.	Will the privatization or outsourcing decision impact current union-represented employees?

Government bureaucracy – The image of government bureaucracy, real or perceived, has been a driving force behind privatization. Due to competitive marketplace pressures, there is widespread belief that private contractors may be more efficient in providing services more quickly and at a lower cost. Many government operations, such as the U.S. Postal Service, had been heavily subsidized and thereby protected from competition. Today, as a privatized entity responsible for its own profits and losses, the Postal Service in the United States competes nicely with United Parcel Service and overnight carriers, such as Federal Express. The Canadian National Railway, privatized in the mid-1990s, notes that "privatization has introduced a new way of doing things, a new mentality within the company and within supply management."[13] The pressure to compete can exert a powerful force on an organization.

Technological savvy – This is often believed to be greater among private contractors, because they are not subject to the vagaries of the governmental budgetary process and they may serve larger territories. This also applies to capital investment. An outside contractor may be able to invest in better equipment and facilities, because its investments are not under as much public scrutiny.

Flexibility – Flexibility may also be greater among private contractors, because they have more freedom to adjust the working hours of their employees and their staffing levels. It is often difficult to eliminate government jobs. Thus, private contractors may be better able to respond to changes in demand.

Political considerations – These considerations loom large in many public organizations, which are under the constant surveillance of the public eye. For example, bringing in competition can be viewed positively. On the other hand, the jobs of public employees may be at stake. This could create unpopular decisions, especially if local people lose jobs and the private contractor is not in a position to create new jobs in the area.

These are some of the factors leading to the increasing popularity of privatization. While privatization is really another form of the make or buy decision, a number of unique considerations exist, simply because of the public scrutiny involved.

Additional Value Enhancement Strategies in Outsourcing

To make a contribution to outsourcing, the purchasing and supply management function must be involved in the outsourcing process. Frequently, however, purchasing is not involved in outsourcing in any meaningful way. While there are indicators that this is changing — purchasers indicate that their involvement has increased and is expected to increase more — it is incumbent upon purchasing to ensure that it becomes involved early in outsourcing decisions. This section explores several issues in outsourcing that relate to purchasing: outsourcing purchasing's non-value-added activities, purchasing's involvement in outsourcing decisions, and outsourcing the purchasing function.

Automate and Outsource Non-Value-Adding Purchasing Activities

It seems that purchasers have long been battling for their function to be viewed as more strategic. One of the reasons that purchasing has not been viewed as strategic is because of all the paper-pushing and clerical-type work that many buyers perform. One way to enhance the value that purchasing adds to an organization is to eliminate the repetitive, non-value-added tasks so that buyers can focus on value-adding activities. The strong move toward this throughout the 1990s continues today. Some administrative work can be eliminated through the use of purchasing cards; more automatic data capture, through bar coding and improved inventory management systems; and more automatic replenishment. Some of these activities that cannot be eliminated can be outsourced. In the total cost of ownership example presented earlier in this chapter, the organization outsourced all of the ordering of materials to its suppliers. The supplier, who is doing the ordering now, ultimately would have had to handle the order anyway. By using proactive purchasing approaches such as integrated supply, purchasers can demonstrate that they are interested in adding value, rather than holding on to work. The time freed from clerical activities can be used in more proactive ways, such as improving cost management and forming better working relationships with key suppliers.

Purchasing Involvement in Outsourcing Decisions

As found in a study by Ellram and Maltz,[14] purchasing is more likely to be involved in outsourcing of nonstrategic activities than strategic activities. How can purchasing increase its level of meaningful involvement? There is no right answer that applies in all situations. The right way to increase involvement depends on the culture of the organization, the current status of purchasing, and top management support. Case studies on purchasing's involvement show that the best way to get involved in outsourcing varies widely.

Take the case of the organization that used total cost of ownership analysis to justify its outsourcing of maintenance, repair, and operating supply items. Purchasing was able to increase its level of involvement because of the excellent business case that it built for the integrated supply decision. Top management was so impressed with purchasing's comprehensive evaluation of outsourcing that it decided that purchasing should be involved in all of the organization's outsourcing decisions.

In the case of Nynex/Bell Atlantic, a consultant found that the organization had a major opportunity to improve its purchasing and outsourcing processes. With that directive and strong support from the CEO, a new vice president of purchasing was hired and given the full support of top management. Though the "old" purchasing function at Nynex/Bell Atlantic had not been involved in outsourcing, the CEO would no longer approve any outsourcing decisions without purchasing's participation in the analysis. The CEO even went so far as to make functions start their outsourcing analyses over from the beginning, with purchasing taking the lead. Such a powerful transformation is only possible with top management support. The pressure of deregulation on the phone industry, just like the competitive pressure the Canadian National Railway felt when it was privatized, overcame many cultural barriers that had historically impeded purchasing's involvement.

Glaxo Wellcome PLC was in a different position. As a highly profitable manufacturer of pharmaceuticals, it was not facing great pressures, but rather it was facing a tremendous opportunity to improve. The group director of purchasing took a different approach: he trained and educated his people in the latest techniques and used a "soft-sell" approach. He positioned purchasing as "internal consultants" to help people spend their money better. This approach took much longer, but again, it was effective given the culture of the company.

Outsourcing the Purchasing Function

There are no "sacred cows" when it comes to outsourcing. Someone has outsourced virtually every function or activity within an organization. So why not outsource purchasing? Shell Oil Company has done that in a way, by moving the purchasing organization into a shared services group and treating purchasing as a profit center. The purchasing group can take on business outside of the Shell Companies, and the Shell Companies can bypass purchasing by using a third party or performing its own purchasing. This initiative began in 1995, and it continues to be successful. Shell Services Company has worked hard to make purchasing an area of core competence.

During 1998, there was an announcement that United Technologies (UT) had outsourced all of its purchasing activities to IBM Services. While UT did not outsource all of its purchasing, the contract is reportedly worth hundreds of millions of dollars and covers all maintenance, repair, and operating supplies at all facilities. In short, it appears to cover all purchases except those that directly affect the final product. Why would an organization choose to outsource purchasing? Returning to the steps in the outsourcing process, UT clearly believed that the purchase of routine, nonproduction items was not strategic. It also believed that these purchases were not a strength for UT — someone else, in this case, IBM, could do it better. Why? Because such purchases are IBM Services' core competency. These events should make all purchasers and all functions within an organization pause to think, and ask the questions:

- Is what our function does strategic, and is it core to the organization's success?
- If so, am I sure of this or biased by my own perspective?
- If not, is our function within the organization so good at this activity from both a cost and a service standpoint that it would be

hard for an outsider to perform it better? Do we add hard-to-imitate value?

- Is our function constantly improving processes and eliminating non-value activities?

If a function cannot answer yes to all of these questions, it is a potential candidate for outsourcing. One way for purchasers to reduce the likelihood that they will be outsourced is to add significant value to an organization. It is possible to position purchasing as an expert in all types of buying, so that those in the organization interested in outsourcing or those wanting to get more value for their budgets will call on purchasing for its expertise.

Purchasing's Contribution to the Outsourcing Process

Purchasing and supply management's area of expertise is buying. A critical factor in any outsourcing or make or buy decision is understanding how to buy: how to develop clear specifications or statements of work; how to identify alternatives; how to assess a provider's ability to meet its promises; how to negotiate; how to develop a contract; and how to manage the relationship on an ongoing basis. These are all areas of unique expertise for purchasing and supply management. Purchasing and supply management must sell its ability to add value in these areas, or it risks being left out of key outsourcing decisions. Supply management should not be involved in outsourcing only after the decision to outsource has been made. It may be too late to add significant value at that point. Purchasing and supply management must be involved when the strategy is being formulated, so that it can help formulate the strategy and assess creative alternatives, as was the case with the Nynex/Bell Atlantic construction example presented earlier in this chapter. Outsourcing should be viewed as an opportunity for proactive buyers, not a threat.

Key Points

1. Outsourcing (the make or buy decision) has strategic implications for the organization, and it should always first be assessed from a strategic perspective.

2. Once a strategic assessment has been made, the outsourcing process involves a feasibility assessment, determination of need, and a total cost of ownership analysis concerning the various scenarios. The total cost of ownership assessment should consider break-even points between alternatives and a sensitivity analysis.
3. Once implemented and in place, an outsourcing decision should always be followed by a post-audit to determine how successful it was, whether modifications are required, and what can be learned for future outsourcing analyses.
4. Privatization, where government services are turned over to private contractors, is increasing throughout the world. It closely mirrors outsourcing in philosophy, benefits, and execution.
5. Purchasing and supply management should view outsourcing as a value-enhancing activity, by using it to reduce or eliminate its own non-value-added processes.
6. The skills of an excellent buyer are directly translatable to support make or buy/outsourcing analysis and execution. It is the responsibility of purchasing and supply management to make these skills and their availability known to support the organization.

Questions for Review

1. What are some of the common mistakes that organizations make in outsourcing?
2. Do you believe that the outsourcing decision is strategic in nature? Why or why not?
3. What are some of the key risks/considerations in outsourcing?
4. How does total cost of ownership analysis support the outsourcing decision-making process?
5. What is meant by the term "privatization," and what is the impetus for privatization?
6. Should all or part of the purchasing function be outsourced? Justify your answer.

For Additional Information

Bernasconi, T.W. "The Latest Trends in Outsourcing," *The Source*, Spring 1996, p. 4.

Burt, D.N. and R.L. Pinkerton. *Strategic Proactive Procurement*, AMACOM, NY, 1996, pp. 96-105.

Dixon, L. and A. Porter-Millen. *JIT II*, Cahners Publishing, Boston, MA, 1994.

Ellram, L.M. and A. Maltz. "TCO in the Outsourcing Decision," *International Journal of Logistics Management*, (6: 2), 1995, pp. 55-66.

Johnson, P.F. and M.R. Leenders. "Make or Buy Alternatives in Plant Disposition Strategies," *International Journal of Purchasing and Materials Management*, (33: 2), Spring 1997, pp. 20-26.

Venkatesan, R. "Strategic Sourcing: To Make or Not to Make?" *Harvard Business Review*, (70), November-December 1992, pp. 98-107.

Endnotes

1. Raedels, A. *The Purchasing Process*, The National Association of Purchasing Management, Tempe, AZ, 2000.
2. Fine, C. *Clockspeed*, Perseus Books, Inc., Reading, MA, 1998.
3. Bernasconi, T.W. "The Latest Trends in Outsourcing," *The Source*, Spring 1996, p. 4.
4. Bernasconi, 1996.
5. Prahalad, C.K. and G. Hamel. "The Core Competence of the Organization," *Harvard Business Review*, (68), May-June 1990, pp. 79-90.
6. Quinn, J.B. and F.G. Hilmer. "Strategic Outsourcing," *Sloan Management Review*, (35), Summer 1994, pp. 43-55.
7. Dozbaba, M.S. "Are We In or Out?" *Purchasing Today®*, April 1999, pp. 54-55.
8. *IBM 1998 Annual Report*.
9. Williamson, O.E. *The Economic Institutions of Capitalism*, Free Press, New York, NY, 1985.

10. Ellram, L.M. and A. Maltz. *Outsourcing: Implications for Supply Management*, Center for Advanced Purchasing Studies, Tempe, AZ, 1996.
11. Ellram and Maltz, 1996.
12. Ellram and Maltz, 1996.
13. Gallant, R.A. and D. Dansereau. "Leverage Your Suppliers' Contribution to Cost Reduction," *Proceedings of the 1997 NAPM International Purchasing Conference*, NAPM, Tempe, AZ, 1997.
14. Ellram and Maltz, 1996.

CHAPTER 2

LEASE VERSUS BUY ANALYSIS AND OTHER LEVERAGING TOOLS

What are the cash flow implications of financing decisions?

Chapter Objectives

- To understand the purpose of leasing and the major types of leasing arrangements
- To identify the various types of lessors
- To compare the pros and cons of leasing versus buying an asset
- To determine when present value analysis is required
- To be familiar with major legal requirements and regulations that relate to leasing
- To be aware of some of the major financing and leveraging options available that relate to purchasing

Introduction

As organizations become increasingly focused on cash flow, there is growing recognition that many purchasing decisions have a significant and direct impact on cash flow and shareholder value. Seventy-six percent of CEOs in a recent survey expect purchasing and supply management to contribute to shareholder value.[1] This chapter explores some of the types of decisions that purchasers make that affect an organization's cash flow, and it begins by focusing on the lease or buy decision in purchasing capital equipment. This is a responsibility that may be shared by purchasing and supply management (PSM) and finance, or it may be the sole responsibility of one or the other.

What is Leasing?

A lease is a contract in which one party (the lessee) has use and possession of an asset owned by another party (the lessor) for a period of time in return for a monetary payment. The lessee makes scheduled payments (usually monthly) to the lessor. The lessor typically makes a profit on the difference between the rental payments and how much it cost the lessor to purchase the asset.

Lessees do not own the assets, but they "rent" them from the lessor. Lessees are permitted to claim rental payments made on such assets as expenses on the organization's income statement. At the end of the lease term, the lessee may have the option to purchase the asset, return it to the lessor, or renew the lease for a longer time period, depending on the lease contract and the needs at that time. The lessee could be an organization of any size, providing a product or service in the public or private sector. As consumers, people are most familiar with leasing arrangements for automobiles. In business, leases may extend to all types of capital equipment and real estate, including personal computers, automobiles, copiers, office space, and equipment used in production.

Types of Leasing Arrangements

The major types of leasing arrangements are presented in the following paragraphs.

Operating Lease

Operating leases are used by organizations to satisfy internal customer needs or to facilitate business operations. Frequently, operating leases satisfy short-term requirements, and they are used for a period of time considerably shorter than the asset's useful life. They are used in cases where capital-intensive equipment is required for short periods of time or is subject to rapid obsolescence. Because of these characteristics, the leasing organization is not interested in owning the equipment. Rental of an automobile for a week is an example of this type of lease. American Express leases all of its personal computers

(PCs) for a three-year term because it does not want to own them due, in part, to rapid obsolescence.

Financial or Capital Lease

This type of lease runs for the full life of the equipment, and it is typically entered into for financial considerations, where the lessee seeks to gain financial leverage and related long-term financial benefits. It is an alternative to a loan, providing more service and/or asset disposition at the end of the lease period. A financial or capital lease is represented as an asset on the lessee's books just as an asset that it owns would be represented. There are two major types of financial leases:

Full Payout – With a full payout lease, the lessee pays the full purchase price, plus interest charges, maintenance, insurance, and administrative costs. It is basically a way of financing the entire capital acquisition.

Partial Payout – A partial payout lease gives the lessee credit for the residual value of the leased item after the lease period is completed. The lessee pays the difference between the original purchase price and the resale value, plus interest charges. Some automobile leases, where the automobile is turned in at the end of the lease period, are examples of this type of lease. This type of lease is riskier than an operating lease, because an unknown amount will be due at the end of the lease term, depending on how well the leased asset retained its value.

Lease/Purchase

Under a lease/purchase contract, the lessee has the option to purchase the equipment at the end of the lease or at specific time intervals. This option is typically exercised at the end of the lease. The purchase price represents the residual value of the asset, and it may be determined at the initial lease signing or based on market value at the time the asset is purchased. Purchasing an automobile at the end of a three-year lease is an example of this alternative.

Leveraged Lease

A leveraged lease is one that involves a third-party lessor that buys the asset from an equipment manufacturer and leases it to another organization. Leveraged leases are usually formed because of the unique tax arrangements and borrowing power the lease provides the lessor. Typical lessors are large investors, such as insurance companies, pension funds, or investment groups. There are brokers who match potential investors with lessees. The lender's debt is primarily secured by an asset and to some extent by the financial capacity of the lessee.

Master Lease

A master lease is similar to a blanket order contract, except that it applies specifically to leases. A master lease uses predetermined and negotiated terms and conditions for various leased equipment over a specified time period. In general, a master lease fits best with operating-type leases where equipment needs are for shorter time periods. A master lease allows the purchaser to negotiate set terms and conditions, and when different short-term needs arise, merely negotiate price and length of use. In addition, a purchaser can negotiate rates for a category of equipment and extend master lease terms to all the equipment. For example, if an organization agrees to lease forklifts from a local equipment dealer, the terms and conditions of the standard lease might also apply to the pickup trucks it decides to lease at a later date.

Dry Lease/Wet Lease

Dry/wet leases originated in the aircraft industry. These leases are designed to address the amount of service provided under the lease arrangement. A dry lease, also known as a straight lease, provides only for financing. A wet lease includes financing, as well as fuel and maintenance for the piece of equipment.

Sale and Leaseback

In a sale and leaseback arrangement, the owner of a piece of equipment or property sells the asset to a second party, and then leases it back. The primary reason for this type of lease is to generate capital. Proceeds from the sale of the equipment or property can be put to alternate uses, while the asset continues to be used on a leased basis. Sale and leaseback provides a good way for an organization to obtain needed capital, while maintaining the use of the asset. Like a leveraged lease, or a loan, it is essentially a financing arrangement that allows the lessee to experience cash outflows (payments) monthly, rather than as a lump sum.

Other Types of Leases

Methods of leasing vary greatly, and they are limited only by manufacturers' or other lessors' marketing creativity. Offers such as "pre-trading" automobiles or leasing land and buildings for long periods carry the same fundamental principle. The lessor seeks to increase the sale of equipment and/or make a profit on the difference between the cost of the asset and the payments received, while the lessee seeks to minimize cash outlay. Thus, cash flow is the key motivator for the lessee. The latter may need cash or see more attractive options for available capital. Opportunities that allow both parties to meet these needs can constitute a leasing arrangement.

Lease Options

Options on leases can include service additions for equipment, maintenance, software, or upgrades to newer models. The structure of these agreements will be favorable to the lessor. Thus, when reviewing options, the lessee should be aware that the costs for these additions are being rolled into the equipment lease, restricting future flexibility. Also, the equipment owner may restrict what type and brand of enhancements may be allowed on or used in conjunction with the leased equipment. Frequently, such enhancements may reduce the lessee's burden of managing and maintaining the leased assets. These trade-offs must be considered.

Types of Lessors

Third-Party Lessors

Third-party lessors produce no products. Rather, they purchase equipment from manufacturers and, in turn, lease the equipment. Third-party lessors, sometimes referred to as *full-service lessors*, include organizations or individuals who find the returns from this type of investment attractive. They make a profit on the difference between lease payments received and the total cost of the asset. An example of this is a farm equipment dealership that purchases equipment from companies such as John Deere and Case, and then leases the equipment to farmers.

Manufacturers

Manufacturers that make high-technology or high-cost products often find that sales can be increased by offering leasing options. For example, the high cost and potential obsolescence of large computers can make them more desirable to users as leased items. Thus, manufacturers often become lessors of their products. Leasing can be a mechanism for managing demand and moving products, such as new, luxury automobiles, into the marketplace. It is not unusual to see brands such as Lexus, Mercedes, and Jaguar offer leasing options. Because there is no alternate source for the same brand of product, this type of lease is normally referred to as a *captive lease*.

Banks and Investment Firms

Banks operate as lessors in a fashion similar to that of third-party lessors. Typically, banks put up a portion of the capital (15 to 30 percent), borrow the remainder, and use the lessee's payments to cover the costs of borrowing, plus profit. For example, GE Capital has partnered with truck manufacturers and tire dealers to provide lease financing for industrial trucks. Fleet Equipment Corp., a truck manufacturer, has seen a shift in leasing from 5 percent of trucks in 1989 to 97 percent of trucks in 1997.[2]

Internal Lessor

Leasing arrangements can also be made within an organization, particularly in large multidivisional or multinational organizations. Investment decisions in one area of the organization might be maximized by purchasing and leasing equipment elsewhere within the organization. Also, equipment produced by one division might be offered for lease within the organization itself.

Other Lessors

At times, institutional investors and/or wealthy individuals may form financial consortiums to supply capital for leasing arrangements. The investors put up a portion (10 to 20 percent) of the purchase price, and financing is obtained on the remainder. The debt is secured through lease payments. The lessee can benefit through receiving lower lease rates, because the individual lessors (who put up only a fraction of the money) claim tax deductions on the entire cost of the equipment. Therefore, to get quality leases, the lessor is willing to provide favorable rates.

Considerations in a Lease or Buy Decision

A number of factors weigh for and against a decision to lease versus purchase a piece of equipment.

Inflation

As a general rule, leasing is a more costly way to obtain a piece of equipment than purchasing because, in addition to covering finance charges, the lessor bears all risks associated with ownership, including inflation. This risk is consequently reflected as a cost component of lease payments. Throughout the 1990s, when inflation was low, this issue was not as important. Lessors often estimate inflation based on the going interest rate for investments that cover a similar period of time.

Obsolescence

By leasing rather than buying a piece of capital equipment, the risk of obsolescence is reduced or eliminated for the lessee. Lessees can negotiate leases that include provisions to have the leased equipment replaced by new or updated models. However, because the lessor bears the risk of equipment obsolescence, it will likely charge a premium above the purchase price for bearing that risk. As stated earlier in this chapter, the high level of obsolescence of personal computers is one of the factors motivating American Express to lease all of its PCs.

Maintenance Services

The lessor bears the cost of maintenance in most leases. This may include initial delivery charges and installation for a piece of equipment. This frees the lessee from administration and provides properly trained labor to maintain the equipment. Maintenance becomes particularly important if the item is complex. Some lessors own and operate their own production and repair shops, and they will generally provide expert service. Often, as a provision of the lease, the lessor provides alternate equipment during any extended downtime. This may be a significant benefit over ownership to the lessee.

Excess Wear and Tear

Some leases include substantial penalties for exceeding a specified amount of usage, or they charge for wear and tear on the equipment. For example, most automobile leases include a maximum number of miles that are allowed during the lease period (generally averaging 12,000 miles per year), after which the lessee may have to pay substantial per-mile penalties. Projected usage versus allowed usage is an important consideration in the economics of lease versus buy decisions.

Capital/Budget Considerations

One of the chief advantages of leasing is that it makes capital available for other, more profitable purposes. A large outlay of capital is replaced by smaller regular payments as the asset is used. On the other hand, the total leasing charges over the life of the equipment normally exceed the cost of the equipment, for the reasons mentioned previously. Although leasing is usually more costly than purchasing in the long run, this must be weighed against the need for the asset when funds are limited or when alternate opportunities for use of those funds are available.

Administrative Overhead

A lease might eliminate the need for extensive record-keeping and asset management, thereby reducing the administrative overhead expenses related to the leased asset. As with other decisions to outsource, the lease cost is known, fixed, and may be inclusive. The cost structure is simple, freeing administrative time to concentrate on the organization's value-added activities.

Reimbursement from Third Parties

Many equipment manufacturers sell leasing contracts to third parties. This is most common in leveraged leasing situations in which the manufacturer or equipment provider is not interested in collection activities. Payments by the lessee are then made to a third party, who pays the manufacturer. The lease may be sold outright, so that the manufacturer receives a lump sum for the lease at the time of sale. Alternatively, the lease may be administered by a third party that collects a fee for handling payments.

Interest

If a purchaser is considering buying rather than leasing equipment, interest costs on the financing must be considered. Rates and the burden of long-term debt may make the purchase of equipment less attractive. A purchaser should always compare the present value of leasing versus buying in assessing the attractiveness of any lease situation. An overview of present value analysis is discussed later in this chapter.

Ownership Benefits

Lessees can be restricted as to how they use leased equipment, and they may be required to provide lessors with access to the equipment upon request. By owning rather than leasing equipment, the purchaser benefits by having complete control of the asset and the ability to use the equipment as he or she pleases. This also includes the ability to add off-brand components (for example, external disc drives from another manufacturer) and to use non-branded maintenance and repair parts. Although ownership carries the burden of disposing of the asset at the end of its useful life, or when it is no longer needed, the owner enjoys the benefits of any residual value. In addition, the asset might provide value to the organization for years after it has been fully depreciated. An example of this is a piece of equipment used to sort and process fliers for direct mail. While this asset may be leased for five years, an organization may be able to use it productively for 10 or more years.

Limitations of Sources of Supply

When suppliers are limited, leasing offers an alternative to purchasing. By considering leasing, a purchaser may negotiate financing with a number of lessors and then choose the best option. Also, considering leasing may entice the supplier to provide a better offer to sell the equipment than might otherwise have been presented. The act of increasing competition might lead to better procurement.

Balance Sheet Considerations

Leasing can make an organization's balance sheet appear stronger than it would be if the equipment were financed. Because most types of leases are shown as an expense on the income statement within the period the lease payment is made, no debt is shown on the balance sheet. When financing an asset, the amount financed appears as a liability until it is paid off. In addition, the value of the purchased asset is shown as an asset on the balance sheet. This asset increases the organization's base of invested capital. A leased asset does not appear on the balance sheet as long as it is an operating lease. Thus, use of leased assets may allow the organization to show a greater return on assets than it would if the assets were owned, by understating the assets used to create income. Given equal profits and the same assets, the organization that leases its assets will show a higher return on assets.

Cash Flow Analysis

Purchase and lease options can cause different effects on cash flow, depending on tax implications and the structure of the lease payments. Generally, leasing rather than buying enhances the immediate cash flow of the lessee by delaying payments into the future. Cash flow has been an area of greater concern for many organizations since the mid-1990s, receiving more attention than previously.

Depreciation

Typically, the owner of the asset has the ability to depreciate the asset. The lessee forgoes the opportunity to depreciate the asset in exchange for the other benefits of leasing. A primary benefit for the lessee is the ability to recognize lease payments as an expense of the current period, as discussed below.

Tax Considerations

Except in the case of financial/capital leases, lease payments are classified as operating expenses. As such, lease payments are completely deductible from taxable income, while owned equipment must be depreciated over the asset's useful life. The lessee may realize tax savings if lease payments exceed allowable depreciable amounts.

Operating Costs

Costs to be considered include the utility, energy, air, environmental compliance, maintenance, water, and labor costs required to use the asset. Special licenses and permits may be needed, as in the case of trucks used in interstate commerce. The administrative costs of monitoring these activities can be minimized through various leasing arrangements.

Life of the Asset

By purchasing rather than leasing an asset, the purchaser has control over the asset throughout its entire life, not just for the lease term. An asset, when fully depreciated, may still provide value to the owner in excess of its residual value. Some assets, such as land, buildings, precious metals, and precious stones, may even appreciate over time.

Residual Value

When a lease term has ended, the lessee does not own the equipment and, therefore, is precluded from reaping any benefit from the residual value that the asset may have in the marketplace. The purchaser should be aware of the relationship between allowable depreciation and residual value for the type of equipment being leased.

Customization of Asset

Because the lessee does not own the piece of leased equipment, the equipment cannot be modified or altered without the permission of the lessor. This condition may also extend to the addition of accessories that interact with the equipment.

Early Termination

When entering into a leasing agreement, a purchaser should fully understand the implications of early termination, should that become desirable or necessary. Termination options become more important the longer the life of the lease. These options may be so expensive that they significantly limit the attractiveness of lease termination.

Payment Schedules

Payment schedules show the due dates for lease payments and are useful in preparing cash-flow analyses. This information is essential in determining the present value of various financing and lease versus buy options.

Insurance

When entering into a lease, insurance requirements should be fully understood. For example, which organization will be responsible for insurance and which one will benefit from any insurance payoff if the assets are damaged, destroyed, or stolen?

Company/Organization Policy

Many organizations maintain formal or informal policies regarding leasing. In high-tech industries, for example, there is a tendency to lease because of the fast pace of technological changes. Organizations with a high rate of growth may also have policies that favor leasing to minimize debt and increase working capital. PSM must be familiar with such requirements.

Term of Lease

The length of the lease is determined by contract, and it reflects the time the asset will be needed. Some leases are open-ended, and they can be canceled following a formal notification period.

Emergency Situations

Leasing can provide equipment for short-term requirements. If a particular piece of equipment is temporarily out of service, leased equipment can provide operating continuity. If funds are not approved or if products do not justify short-term capital outlay, leased equipment may fill the need, even if leasing is more expensive than purchasing equipment in the long run.

Leasing can also provide access to equipment that is in short supply or that has long leadtimes. Lessors may have focused on these market conditions or, through leverage with suppliers, have these assets available for lease.

Present Value

Everyone knows that money has a "time value." A dollar is worth more today than five years from now, because that dollar could be invested or otherwise spent now so that the benefits of that dollar could be enjoyed today. This amount is considered "the opportunity cost of capital."

Whenever various financing options are under consideration — whether it is lease versus buy, or different payment terms — present value (PV) analysis may be a consideration. Specifically, if the payment terms extend a year or more or if the dollar value is significant, the present value of the alternatives should be considered. Due to the time value of money, the present value of money to be paid out in the future is less than the PV of that money today.

To illustrate, suppose that an organization was going to purchase a piece of office equipment. If the organization decided to lease, it would pay $3,000 today and $4,000 at the end of year one and the end of year two.

The present value of $10,000 paid today is $10,000 in today's dollars. Likewise, under the lease alternative, the $3,000 paid today is worth $3,000 in today's dollars. But the $4,000 paid at the end of years one and two are worth less than $4,000 in today's dollars, because the organization had the opportunity to use those dollars for a year or two before making the payments.

The present value factor is shown as:

$PVF_n = 1/(1 + i)^n$

Where i = effective interest rate or cost of capital

      n = number of periods until payment is received

If the organization's cost of capital (interest cost to borrow money/finance debt) is 10 percent, then:

$PVF1 = 1/(1 + 0.10)^1 = 0.9091$

$PVF2 = 1/(1 + 0.10)^2 = 0.8264$

Thus, $4,000 one year from now is worth (in today's dollars):

    $4,000 x 0.9091 = $3,636.40

And the payment two years from now is worth (in today's dollars):

    $4,000 x 0.8264 = $3,305.60

Add the present value of the three cash outflows together:

    $3,000 + $3,636.40 + $3,305.60 = $9,942

Thus, the present value of these cash outflows is worth less than $10,000 paid in cash today.

This would not be the only consideration. Tax laws, residual value, and other issues would also play a role.

A more detailed explanation of present value analysis is beyond the scope of this book, but any basic finance textbook can provide an adequate explanation. The concept of present value analysis is to consider the time and amount of future payments, and then to "revalue" them to today's dollars using the buying organization's opportunity cost of capital. This calculation can be done quite easily in most spreadsheet packages. For example, Microsoft Excel includes a function called PV that allows the user to input cash flows and an interest rate (representing the opportunity cost of capital) in order to determine the present value of a payment stream. When unsure about the appropriateness of PV analysis for a given situation, purchasers should contact finance or accounting. They should have years of training in financial matters, and they may be the ones that perform the actual analysis.

Legal and Accounting Considerations

The financial, tax, and legal implications for organizations involved in leasing are generally covered by the Uniform Commercial Code (Article 2A) and the Financial Accounting Standards Board (FASB) (Statement Number 13). Major topics under each are mentioned below. FASB references to capital leases apply to financial leases as previously described in this chapter.

Uniform Commercial Code 2A – Leasing

Article 2A of the Uniform Commercial Code covers leases and legal implications for merchants. The section has five parts:

Part 1: General Provisions
Part 2: Formation and Construction of Lease Contract (includes offers, performance, warranties, and casualties to identified goods)
Part 3: Effect of Lease Contract (includes enforceability, title, sub-lease, liens on assets or equipment, and creditor rights)
Part 4: Performance of Lease Contract: Repudiated, Substituted, and Excused (includes assurance of performance, anticipatory repudiation, excused or substituted performance, and irrevocable promises)
Part 5: Default (includes notices of default, lessor/lessee remedies, waiver of objections, liquidation of damages, cancellation, and termination)

Purchasers should be aware of these provisions and their implications on leasing contracts.

FASB-13

The Financial Accounting Standards Board details proper methods for recording and accounting transactions in business. Statement 13 deals with leases and lists appropriate transactions for lessors, lessees, and third parties in various types of leasing arrangements. A lease is described as an agreement conveying the right to use plant, property, or equipment for an agreed upon period of time.

FASB differentiates between two basic kinds of leases. The first is a capital lease, which is also known as a financial lease. Under this type of contract, the benefits and risk of ownership are transferred to the lessee. In this case, the property or equipment should be recorded as an acquisition by the lessee and as a sale by the lessor. This is similar to a financial or leveraged lease, which was described earlier in this chapter. FASB considers all other types of leases as operating leases, which are essentially treated like the rental of property. Under an operating lease, neither an asset nor an obligation is recorded on the lessee's balance sheet. Rather, rental payments are shown as an expense on the income statement in the period in which they occurred.

To quote FASB Statement 13, "If at its inception a lease meets one or more of the following four criteria, the lease shall be classified as a capital lease by the lessee. Otherwise, it shall be classified as an operating lease." The four conditions are:

1. The lease contains a bargain purchase or bargain renewal option.
2. The lease transfers ownership of the property to the lessee by the end of the lease term. Thus, the intent of the lease is ownership, and should be reflected as such.
3. The lease term is equal to 75 percent or more of the estimated economic life of the leased property.
4. The present value at the beginning of the lease term of the minimum lease payments equals or exceeds 90 percent of the fair market value (FMV) of the leased property at the inception of the lease (the FMV of the property to be reduced by any investment tax credit or energy credit retained by the lessor prior to determining the 90 percent base).

The standards also discuss a "sales-type" lease, which is used by a manufacturer in order to sell its products. This is similar to a captive lease (described earlier in this chapter). Overall, FASB-13 delineates proper methods of accounting for various types of activities that result from leasing. The standards provide guidance for leasing alternatives and their implications in a financial environment. A purchaser involved in leasing should become aware of these accounting standards and the alternatives to acquisitions that they represent. This may require working with the organization's financial and/or legal staff.

Other Issues

As alternative forms of financing become a more important issue in supplying an organization's assets, legal concerns and the proper recording of activities on financial statements will grow in complexity. Aside from the actual equipment or property itself, decisions will be based more and more on the tax and/or legal implications of the financing options. For this reason, purchasers will need a working knowledge of the issues, as well as professional support from the legal and accounting departments, when choosing an alternative.

Role of PSM in Leasing

The role of PSM in leasing varies among organizations. To the extent that PSM is involved in the capital acquisition process, it should understand the implications of leasing, various types of leases, and how to compare the present value of various financing options. Purchasers who are unfamiliar with leasing and present value analysis should work closely with more experienced purchasers and accounting and legal staff members when presented with various leasing and financing options.

The next section briefly presents some of the other financing and leasing strategies for purchasing. Purchasing's level of involvement and participation in such strategies will vary widely among organizations. It is highly recommended that purchasers do more research prior to becoming involved in any of these options. The bottomline is that all of these strategies represent an approach for influencing the cash flow, and potentially the revenue or cost, of an organization. As such, they are valuable tools.

Other Financing and Leveraging Strategies for Purchases: External Opportunities

Numerous external opportunities are available for gaining leverage. Each carries its own risks and rewards. Each is affected by market conditions outside of the purchaser's control.

Depreciation and Appreciation

Due to market conditions, the value of assets changes over time. For example, in high-tech industries, the value of parts and components is continually declining as new, improved, and often less expensive technologies are introduced.

A purchaser may inadvertently cost his or her organization millions of dollars by holding large inventories of components or materials that are depreciating in value. A large stockpile of finished goods and components cost Apple Computer tens of millions of dollars in 1997, contributing to its disappointing earnings and asset restructuring.[3]

On the other hand, assets and materials may also appreciate in value. For example, with the increases in crude oil prices in the late 1990s, organizations holding large stocks of crude oil and associated products suddenly found that their assets were worth more.

Generally speaking, most organizations do not attempt to hold assets to gain appreciation or depreciation unless they are in the business of buying and selling commodities. Such high-risk strategies are generally handled by a trained professional, such as a commodities trader who constantly monitors the market for fluctuations. This is not something that a purchaser should attempt to dabble in.

Likewise, a purchaser should carefully monitor stocks of essential items that are known to experience a high degree of price volatility. Otherwise, the organization may experience unanticipated depreciation losses and appreciation gains.

Bond and Currency Markets

While it is rare for buyers to be involved in bond markets, purchasers are increasingly involved in foreign currency markets, either directly or indirectly, each time they make a purchase from a source that uses a different currency. As in appreciation and depreciation, this is not an area for purchasers to dabble in. The volatility and risks may be high. Trading in foreign currency in an attempt to make money on short-term market inefficiencies is known as arbitrage, and it is widely considered to be one of the riskiest propositions available. Some companies have trained professionals who do this.

Most companies, such as Johnson & Johnson, ask that buyers consult the U.S. Treasury Department for guidance whenever developing a contract or engaging in a significant transaction that could be denominated in a different currency. Like most major corporations, Johnson & Johnson's goal is to hedge and/or eliminate the risk of currency fluctuations, rather than to let transactions "float," in hopes that the currency will change favorably and the value of the contract with the supplier will appreciate. Figure 2.1 shows what can happen to the value of currency, and the associated value of the purchase, if the exchange rate is simply allowed to float, meaning that the buying organization agrees to pay in local currency. This example shows the high degree of variability that can occur in the price paid. Here, the yen/dollar exchange rate is currently $150 yen/dollar, yielding a price of $33,333 U.S. dollars for an item costing $500,000 yen. If the exchange rate goes to $250 yen/dollar, the firm would pay $20,000 U.S. dollars. On the other hand, if the exchange rate went to $50 yen/dollar, the same transaction would cost the buying organization $100,000 U.S. dollars. Thus, floating exchange rates can be risky.

Two other options are shown in Figure 2.1 — sharing the change in relative currency valuation with the supplier and shifting the risk to the supplier by denominating the transaction in the buyer's currency. The key is not to ignore the risk of currency fluctuation, but to manage it. Some other ways to protect the organization from currency fluctuations include hedging the transaction by purchasing a spot contract for the amount of foreign currency needed to cover the transaction payment. These concepts are presented in more depth in Chapter 8. A *spot contract* is a contract to purchase foreign currency, based on current exchange rates, to meet specific foreign currency needs today. For future transactions, an organization could buy a forward contract, which is valued at today's exchange rate, adjusted for the time value of money. The foreign currency would be "delivered" at an agreed upon date that is planned to meet the needs for future transactions.

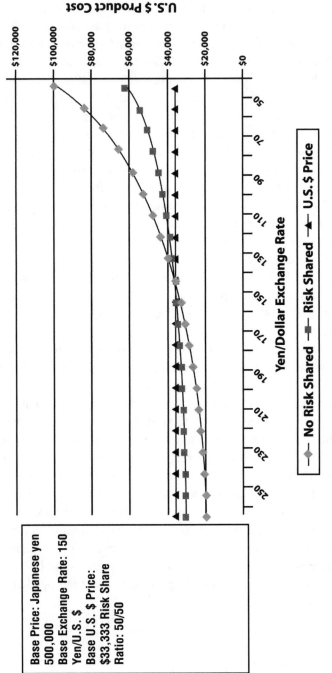

FIGURE 2.1
Foreign Exchange Risk Under Different Currency Agreements

No risk sharing: The transaction is denominated in Japanese yen; the U.S. organization absorbs all the risk of currency fluctuation.

Risk sharing: Changes in the exchange rate of U.S. dollars versus yen are shared 50/50.

U.S. $ Price: The transaction is denominated in U.S. dollars; all risk of currency fluctuation is transferred to the Japanese organization.

Commodity Markets

Openly traded commodities include metals, grains, coffee, crude oil, and similar items in large demand that are easily graded. These markets are known to be extremely volatile. Large companies that trade heavily in these markets, including Cargill, M&M Mars, and Pillsbury, have specialized commodity traders. The traders constantly watch the market and judge whether the organization should buy large amounts (forward buy) for future use and/or appreciation, or if the organization should buy only for current needs (hand-to-mouth buying). These approaches are presented in greater depth in Chapter 8. Again, the valuation changes are based on uncontrollable market factors. If an organization buys large amounts today for future use or resale, it must determine the impact of such a decision on the organization's cash flow and identify whether such a purchase is truly the best investment of the organization's funds.

Regulations and Tax Laws

Regulations and tax laws may dictate an organization's ability to recognize certain expenses for tax reporting purposes. For example, the Internal Revenue Service has established specific rules for recognizing depreciation on buildings and equipment and depletion of wells and mines. These rules and regulations may have little to do with the useful life of the item. Yet, these rules determine when expenses can be recognized for tax reporting purposes, thereby affecting the organization's tax liability and the associated cash flow. Depreciation, amortization, and depletion are non-cash expenses that reduce the organization's reported income, which in turn reduces its tax burden and increases its cash flow. Purchasers should consult with finance personnel to determine the tax and cash flow implications, because the laws are complex and change frequently. This would not affect nonprofit organizations and government entities that do not pay taxes.

Financing Issues

Whenever considering financing options, especially if they extend over a period of time, it is critical to evaluate them on a present value basis. The relative interest rate charged can be a big factor

influencing the decision, with lower interest rates being more attractive. Due to cash flow issues, some organizations are "forced" to
accept very high interest rates for financing, simply because they do
not have the cash or other appropriate financing available.

Suppliers may offer financing for equipment and capital purchases. They may have a low implied interest rate on a high price, as
is frequently the case in the purchase of new automobiles. Or they
may have a low price, but a high rate for financing. The only way to
evaluate the attractiveness of the offer is to assess it on a present
value basis.

Payment terms offered by a supplier should also be evaluated on
the basis of the total package. For example, a supplier may offer different terms and prices as follows:

> Option A: 2%/10, net 30 with a price of $60/unit.
> Option B: Net 90 with a price of $63/unit.

A mistake that organizations make is to immediately go for the
second option, because it has such attractive payment terms. The purchaser must evaluate both offers by equalizing them — either adding
an interest penalty to the item that requires earlier payment or a credit to the item that permits later payment. The offers should be evaluated based on the way that the buying organization will pay the supplier. The evaluation of the offers also needs to consider the organization's opportunity cost of capital. For this example, use 10 percent.
To calculate the value of the discount and allow the bids to be compared on an equal basis, follow these steps:

1. Account for the discount:
    $60/per unit * 0.02 discount = $58.80 unit discounted
2. Equalize the bid terms:
    longest bid term – shortest bid term = days to penalize
    90 days – 10 days = 80 days to penalize
    Note: 10 days is used because it is assumed that the discount is
    taken.
3. Determine the organization's daily cost of annual capital oppor-
    tunity cost of capital:
    10% cost of capital/365 days = 0.0274% or 0.000274

4. Determine the penalty for early payment:
   price for the item the organization would have to pay for earlier
   * days of penalty * daily interest
   $58.80 * 80 * 0.000274 = $1.29 early payment penalty per unit
5. Determine adjusted unit value:
   price of the item the organization would have to pay for earlier +
   early payment penalty
   $58.80 + 1.29 = $60.09

What does this show? Compare the prices of the two options:

> Option A: $60.09 adjusted price
> Option B: $63

Thus, Option A is a better deal. Given the alternative of Option A at 2%/10, net 30, the most the organization should pay for this same item to receive the 90-day terms is $60.09. However, if an organization is cash-constrained, it may still see the 90-day terms as attractive, simply because it has no other options or it has a long cash-to-cash cycle from the time it pays for its production inputs to the time it receives payment from its customers.

Buying Alternatives for Leverage

Buying organizations can take numerous approaches to leverage their purchases in the supply market and with their suppliers.

Centralized Purchasing

In this approach, a centralized purchasing organization combines like purchases of various operating units and leverages the higher volume in order to gain better pricing, terms, service levels, and visibility. Such centralized purchasing is often mandated, in that there are no divisional purchasers or that divisional purchasers buy only unique items. This approach is used at Intel, and it is common in governmental agencies and public institutions.

Corporate Purchasing

Increasingly common today, corporate purchasing is usually a small, separate group of buyers that guides corporate policy and looks for leveraging opportunities throughout the organization. Unlike centralized purchasing, the business units in this type of organization generally have their own purchasing staff, and they can choose whether to use corporate contracts. This approach is used by Stork, NV, a Dutch industrial equipment and service company. The corporate purchasing group must sell its services to the divisions and show benefits to the divisions, or the divisions will continue to purchase autonomously.

Lead Divisional Buying

Like the two previous methods, lead divisional buying leverages common purchases across divisions, combining volume to gain associated improvements in price, terms, service, and market visibility. However, instead of relying on a centralized corporate group, a division takes the lead for a particular purchase. Different divisions manage different purchases, spreading the work across the organization, often with limited or no additional purchasing staff.

In any of the preceding cases, an organization may extend the benefits of volume contracts to its suppliers. In some cases, proactive purchasing organizations, such as the one at American Express, have even negotiated with suppliers to extend such contracts to customers. Others, like General Motors, may extend contract terms to suppliers and customers, but charge a fee or commission.[4]

Group Purchasing Organizations

Group purchasing organizations take a variety of forms and names. Often known as *consortium buying*, these organizations form specifically to leverage the purchasing volume of independent organizations. They may use the corporate purchasing model by hiring a separate, independent group to manage leveraged purchases, or they may use the lead divisional buying approach by spreading primary purchasing responsibility for various items among member companies. The idea of consortium buying originated in government-funded organizations, such as school districts, to leverage volume and expertise in the face of limited resources. However, consortium buying has expanded significantly and grown in popularity in private organizations as well.[5]

All of the preceding approaches represent opportunities for combining the volume of purchases for like items to gain leverage in terms of market visibility, pricing, terms and conditions, service, and associated factors. At the same time, they may reduce the overall administrative burden, because only one source, rather than multiple sources, is investigating the market and negotiating the contract.

Key Points

1. Leasing represents a financing option for capital equipment and other long-term assets.
2. Many forms of leases are available, and each form has different characteristics and different levels of service.
3. There are many types of lessors, and each lessor has its own motivation, from selling equipment, to gaining tax benefits, to earning a profit on the lease as an investment.
4. There are many factors, both qualitative and quantitative, to consider in lease-buy analysis.
5. Cash flow and balance sheet implications are often a primary driver of lease financing.
6. Present value analysis should be used whenever evaluating a lease-buy decision or any type of financing alternative.
7. Numerous other financing and leveraging decisions are made by purchasers, often unwittingly. In general, purchasers should not engage in behavior that puts their organization at risk for significant changes in the value of purchased items.
8. Internally, purchasers can gain significant volume, price, and service leverage by combining like buys.

Questions for Review

1. What is the major difference between an operating lease and a financial or capital lease?
2. How would the motivations of a third-party lessor differ from those of a manufacturer-lessor?

3. How can capital budgeting influence the lease-buy decision?
4. How do balance sheet and cash flow considerations affect the lease-buy decision?
5. What is meant by present value analysis, and how does it affect purchasing decisions?
6. What is the general approach buyers should take in regard to pursuing external opportunities for market leverage?
7. Compare and contrast the various types of buying alternatives to gain leverage.

For Additional Information

Wright, B. "Capital and Its Impact on Organizations." In *The Purchasing Handbook*, R. Kauffman and J. Cavinato (Eds.), New York, NY: MacMillan, 1999.

Endnotes

1. A.T. Kearney. A.T. *Kearney Global Procurement Study*, 1999.
2. Fair, B. "To Lease or Not to Lease," *Modern Tire Dealer*, February 1997, pp. 43-44.
3. Apple Computer. 1997 *Annual Report*.
4. "Ford and GM to Put Supply Operations Online in Rival E-Commerce Ventures," *The Wall Street Journal*, November 3, 1999, p. A4.
5. Hendrick, T.E. *Purchasing Consortiums: Horizontal Alliances among Firms Buying Common Goods and Services — What? Who? Why? How?* Center for Advanced Purchasing Studies, Tempe, AZ, 1997.

CHAPTER 3

INVENTORY CONTROL AND MANAGERIAL ISSUES

What are the underlying managerial issues in inventory control? Why is inventory getting so much attention today? What could organizations do to manage it better, and what are the pitfalls to avoid?

Chapter Objectives

- To explain the purposes of inventory and how inventories are classified
- To discuss inventory management systems and ordering procedures
- To consider stores' management and how inventories are valued and measured for performance
- To reflect on managerial issues of inventory control and their implications for purchasing

What is Inventory?

Inventory refers to the stock of goods and resources that are waiting to be applied to the value-adding activities in an organization. In manufacturing, inventories either contribute to the manufacturing process or become part of the final product. In service, inventories refer to physical goods that will be sold or used during the delivery of services.

In recent years, inventory has developed a bad name among managers, but it serves important functions; if these are forgotten, it can lead to detrimental consequences for the organization. For example, a top manager at a leading manufacturer of semiconductors unilaterally issued an edict to drastically reduce what appeared to be work-in-process (WIP) inventories. These inventories became visible to him after the implementation of enterprise resource planning (ERP). Despite protests from lower-level managers, the edict was carried out and led to dire consequences. The company delivery rate, once over 99 percent, fell to a mere 70 percent. The organization was scrambling to meet deadlines and was losing market share to its competitors. How did this happen? The top manager had eliminated WIP inventories that helped local operations managers to deal with uneven cycle rates among dependent production operations. The level of these necessary inventories had been determined by the local managers after years of experience. As this chapter will consider, inventories, WIP and other types, serve important purposes in organizations. Until purchasers understand them, they cannot eliminate or reduce inventory in a systematic and rational manner.

Why Does Inventory Exist?

Inventories help managers live with the inherent uncertainties that they face in their daily operations. Uncertainties are the result of variations in demand, supply, and internal operations. For instance, a production supervisor may receive a phone call from a customer requesting changes in delivery dates, order sizes, and so on. Another example is a supplier that cannot meet its promised delivery dates. For such instances, inventories exist as a cushion.

A headphone manufacturer, Koss Corp., had been cutting down its inventory since the early 1990s.[1] However, during the holiday season in 1996, the firm was not able to meet market demand due to the lack of inventory. So, CEO Michael Koss ordered significantly increased inventory levels, despite resistance from his managers. The plan has worked so far. The company eliminated the back orders toward the end of 1997. Since then, it has increased fill rates and reduced delivery time from what was once several weeks to the present 48 hours.

Inventories also help operations that include varied performance cycles to coexist. This function is typically referred to as the *decoupling* of operations. For example, inventory allows operations that require longer cycles to be sequenced side-by-side with operations that require shorter cycles. Also, when setup costs are high, inventories make it possible to reduce the number of setups by decoupling the operations. In other words, with the upstream parts inventories, an operation with a high setup can run a large lot to gain maximum cost advantage.

Toyota has used finished goods inventories (finished automobiles) to help maintain leveled production. Because its inventory pull system does not react well to quickly changing demands, its managers created a buffer zone at the finished goods end to protect its internal operations cycles.[2] Further, even if an organization is not engaged in a Toyota-like pull system, inventories of finished goods can help reduce the pressure to meet deadlines. This allows a longer leadtime and subsequent flexibility, which makes the production planning smoother.

An organization incurs transactional costs when placing an order. Such costs include issuing requests for quotation, phone calls, time spent in meetings, time engaged in contracting, and moving goods through transportation. Therefore, larger inventories can help an organization gain economies of scale and reduce the overall price per item. The larger the size of the order, the fewer the number of orders. Also, shipping at a full-truckload rate is much less expensive than shipping at a less-than-truckload rate.

Inventory Classifications

Most organizations use the same general classifications of inventories. The classifications are organized based on the location of the inventory in the value-adding process or the inventory's characteristics based on its purpose.

Raw Materials

A raw material inventory refers to all items that act as input to an organization's value-adding process. These goods, after being received, are transformed before becoming a distinct and identifiable part of the finished good. Components can be considered raw materials that need no further transformation to become a distinct and identifiable part. For a plastic molding company, plastic resin is a raw material and not a component; however, a front-end bumper manufactured by a plastic molding company is both a raw material and a component to an automobile manufacturer.

Work-in-Process Goods

These goods are still moving through the value-adding process; they will eventually become complete, at which point they will become finished goods inventory. Work-in-process goods represent the inventory of materials in a production process. The location of their placement and the rate of their flow through the transformation process are controlled by operations management.

Finished Goods

Such goods refer to the stock of finished and identifiable products. They are typically stored at the factory while awaiting sale and shipment. However, they can include goods held in warehouses owned and managed by the manufacturer or goods maintained on the buyer's plant floor, which are on consignment. At this point, the management of finished goods inventory can exert a significant impact on the organization's finances. For instance, in the era of JIT II, the buying organization often requests suppliers to keep finished goods (that is, finished goods from the supplier's perspective, but raw materials from the buyer's perspective) on the premise that the buyers will be charged when the goods are used. Thus, the management of finished goods, indeed, has become an important strategic consideration.

Supplies

All materials used by an organization that do not become part of the finished goods are referred to as supplies. Cost accounting typically refers to this inventory as indirect material, whereas the material used in the creation of finished goods is referred to as direct material. More specifically, items that are used for the upkeep of the operations, such as light bulbs, machine parts, and lubricating oil, are referred to as maintenance, repair, and operating (MRO) inventories. These items are needed in both manufacturing and service organizations.

Inventory Management Systems

To understand inventory management systems, it is important to differentiate between two key demand environments — independent demand and dependent demand. Many retailers (for example, Sears) operate in an independent demand environment, where the purchase of one item affects only the production of that item. For instance, at Sears, the sale of a refrigerator does not necessarily affect the demand for women's shoes. Therefore, Sears considers refrigerators and women's shoes independent demand inventories.

However, for a refrigerator manufacturer (for example, Whirlpool), the sale of a refrigerator triggers demand for many related or dependent parts. Depending on the model, a refrigerator requires a certain number of door panels, fasteners, trays, compressors, and so on. These subsequent parts and assemblies are dependent on one another — how many of one item is needed affects how many of other items are needed. For example, if one door panel is required, and 10 particular fasteners are required to attach this door to the refrigerator unit, then for every door panel, the company must maintain 10 of these fasteners. The door and the fasteners are now considered dependent demand inventories. Figure 3.1 demonstrates the relationship between independent and dependent demand.

FIGURE 3.1
Independent and Dependent Demand Tree Diagram

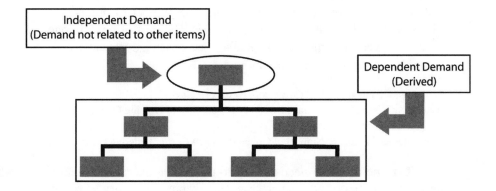

Independent Demand Environment

The complex dynamics between organizations and their markets pose a serious challenge for managers forecasting the demand patterns and determining the size of inventories to maintain. To meet this challenge, many organizations are beginning to rely on electronic data interchange (EDI) for transferring point-of-sale (POS) information to warehouses and to headquarters. For instance, Ahold USA is a large management firm that controls materials for more than 1,000 supermarkets. The firm is connecting its stores to integrate information on demand patterns and subsequent inventory control policies.[3]

However, even with the ready transfer of POS information, the underlying issues of independent demand inventory management remain the same. On the one hand, large orders lead to large inventories, which lead to higher holding costs (including the cost of storage, obsolescence, or deterioration). On the other hand, small orders increase the frequency of ordering, thus increasing ordering costs. The desire to find a balance between the holding cost and the ordering cost has led to the development of a technique called *economic order quantity*.

Economic Order Quantity (EOQ) – EOQ refers to the quantity that corresponds to the minimum point in the total cost curve. In the equation that describes the total cost curve, the dependent and independent variables are cost and quantity, respectively.

The total cost curve includes both the holding cost and the ordering cost. The holding cost is obtained by multiplying the average inventory level by the cost for holding one item for a given year. The ordering cost is computed by multiplying the number of orders in a given year by the cost of placing one order. The cost of holding one item for a year and the cost of placing one order are typically estimated by the accounting department.

Total Cost = Annual Holding Cost + Annual Ordering Cost
Annual Holding Cost = (Average Inventory Level)(Cost of Holding One Item Per
    Year (H))
Annual Ordering Cost = (Number of Orders Per Year)(Cost of Ordering One Lot (S))

Next, the equation needs a way to obtain the average inventory level and number of orders per year. The average inventory level can be computed by dividing the ordering quantity (Q) by 2, assuming that there is a uniform rate of usage. In other words, assume that if a given level of inventory, say Q, is used up every month, the average inventory level is going to be half of Q. Because the monthly average inventory level is Q/2, the annual average inventory level is also Q/2. Then, the number of orders per year is obtained by dividing the total annual demand (D) by the ordering quantity (Q). Replacing the mathematical symbols in the equations shown above produces the following equation for the total cost:

$$\text{Total Cost} = [(Q/2) \times H] + [(D/Q) \times S] = QH/2 + DS/Q$$

EOQ, as shown in Figure 3.2, represents a quantity that signifies an optimum point between the holding cost and the ordering cost. As long as the assumptions hold, it gives a robust estimate for the size of an initial order. The equation for EOQ can easily be obtained by setting the holding cost and the ordering cost equal to each other and solving for Q. In other words, the minimum point on this total cost curve is where the holding cost and the ordering cost intersect:

$$\text{EOQ} = \text{SQRT} \ [2DS/H]$$

FIGURE 3.2

Total Cost Graph

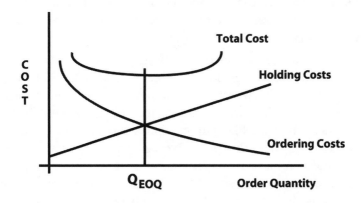

To demonstrate the use of this equation, consider the following conditions:

D = 40,000 units per year
S = $50 per order
H = $0.25 per piece per year

Plugging these numbers into the formula arrives at the following conclusion:

EOQ = SQRT [(2)(40,000)(50)/0.25] = SQRT [16,000,000] = 4,000 units

Inventory Control Systems – There are two basic types of inventory control systems. One is called a fixed order quantity (FOQ) system, and the other is called a fixed time period (FTP) system. In an FOQ system, the size of the order remains fixed, while the time between orders changes, depending on how quickly the items are used up. However, in an FTP system, the time between the orders remains fixed, while the size of the order changes each time, depending on how quickly the items are used up. In an FOQ system, a reorder point triggers the placement of the order, whereas in an FTP system, the regular time intervals trigger the placement of the order. Also, in FTP, the size of the order is derived by a predetermined target inventory level. The order size would bring up the inventory level to the target level at the time of ordering.

Figures 3.3 and 3.4 show how the mechanics of FOQ and FTP work, respectively. Notice that in the FOQ system the order quantities (Q1 and Q2) remain the same, while the time between orders (TBO1 and TBO2) varies. In FTP, however, the periods between orders (P) remain constant, while the inventory positions (IP1, IP2, and so on) vary depending on how quickly the inventory is used up within a period.

When an office worker orders more copy paper whenever the level of white paper goes down to three reams, a form of FOQ is being used. Three reams represent the reorder point, and the size of the order will usually correspond with the bulk discounts offered by the supplier, which are likely to remain fixed over a time period. On the other hand, when this office worker has an agreement with a paper supplier to have its representative visit once every week and bring the level of white paper up to a certain level, a form of FTP is being deployed. In this case, the time between orders is fixed, and each time the size of the order changes, depending on how much white paper was used during the preceding week.

FIGURE 3.3
FOQ System

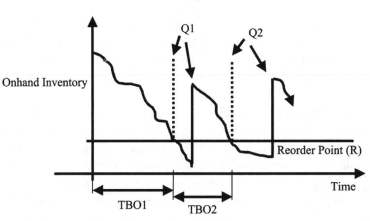

FIGURE 3.4
FTP System

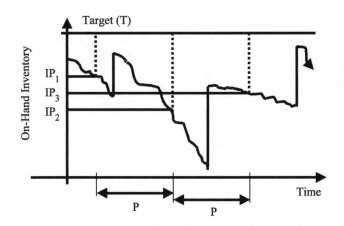

As a side note, putting the reorder point at three reams in the FOQ system would most likely correspond with the point where the rate of usage and the supplier leadtime converge. However, because these don't always converge at the same moment, the office worker knows that there should be some safety stock stashed away to overcome such uncertainties. In the FTP system, safety stock is required for the same reason. However, for this system, the level of required safety stock is generally higher, because the FTP system entails an inherently higher level of uncertainty compared to the FOQ system. In the FOQ system, constant surveillance of the inventory level is required. Whereas in the FTP system, the inventory is checked only at the predetermined time point. The downside of the FOQ system is that it costs more to administer, because it requires a system of constant surveillance.

ABC Inventory Planning – Controlling inventory through counting, ordering, receiving, and storing requires resources. Because resources are limited in most organizations, management must allocate the resources to manage inventory in an optimal way.

Following the Pareto principle, an organization can assume that 20 percent of the inventory controls 80 percent of the value. (This principle was developed by Pareto when he discovered that 20 percent of the citizens in 19th century Milan controlled 80 percent of the wealth.) Therefore, according to ABC inventory planning, inventories should be separated into three categories — high-value items (A), moderate-value items (B), and low-value items (C). Value refers to importance. An item with a low cost but a high volume can be more important than an item with a high cost but a low volume.

A typical breakdown of the inventory based on ABC analysis would result in the following:

- A items make up approximately the top 20 percent of items and 80 percent of dollar usage.
- B items include the next 30 percent of items and 15 percent of dollar usage.
- C items make up the last 50 percent of items and 5 percent of dollar usage.

Amazingly, the breakdowns roughly work out in this way. Once this analysis is done, management should set up appropriate inventory control policies for each of the three categories. For instance, a weekly meeting can focus on A items, while biweekly and monthly meetings can focus on B items and C items, respectively. For example, Office Depot has developed special Web sites for customers with large accounts.[4] These A category customers receive additional attention from the company and are able to purchase products with specific features at specially contracted prices.

Dependent Demand Environment

The focus up to this point has been on when to order inventory and how much to order. These questions were answered by the determination of reorder points and EOQ calculation. However, reorder point and EOQ calculations assumed that all items in inventory were independent of one another and that all items were ordered independently of one another. In an environment of dependent demand (for example, the assembly of computer components, engine assemblies, or furniture assemblies), all items are dependent on other items, and ordering one item has an immediate impact on the ordering of other items. The system that allows operations managers to answer the questions of when and how much of a certain item to order in a dependent demand environment is called material requirements planning (MRP).

The MRP system includes three types of inputs. The inputs, as shown in Figure 3.5, are the master production schedule, which contains information about demand projections; inventory information; and a bill of materials (BOM), which contains detailed information about a product's composition (parts and subassemblies). The output of the MRP system is the report that helps managers of internal manufacturing operations decide what to make, how much to make, and when to make it. This report also informs purchasing about what to order, how much to order, and when to order from suppliers.

The complexity of MRP can be solved through the deployment of a computer-based MRP system. This will permit operations managers to focus more on production planning and control than on tracing the movement of materials. However, there have been problems regarding the deployment of MRP. Most notably, MRP does not work well when it is not integrated throughout the whole manufacturing operation. Without the support of top management, it has no chance of working to its full capability.

FIGURE 3.5
How MRP Coordinates Information

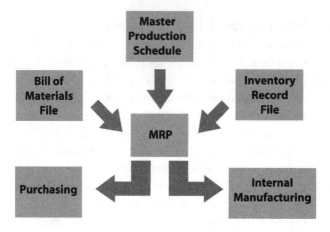

As a side note, MRP II (or manufacturing resource planning) takes the planning process beyond a one-plant operation to an organizationwide operation. In particular, it integrates operations across several plants and plant operations with finance to better manage inventories and their financial values (for example, dollar values of inventories, backlogs, and overhead allocations). Recently, ERP has expanded the functions of MRP and MRP II to integrate not only the plant operation and finance but also human resources, logistics, and distribution. A growing number of organizations boast successes after the implementation of ERP. For example, Findings Inc., a jewelry manufacturer based in Keene, New Hampshire, reported a 66.7 percent increase in its productivity (that is, the number of goods produced monthly) after implementing an ERP system.[5] However, ERP systems can be quite expensive and time-consuming, and they offer no guarantees of success. For example, one company spent more than $23 million on a SAP system, the most popular ERP brand, but the implementation had not yet been completed.[6] Other companies have been known to spend more than $200 million to implement ERP with no clear results.

Inventory Stores Management

Once inventories arrive at an organization, they are stored on the premises. Control of these inventories essentially becomes a problem of communications management. The complexity of this problem is directly proportional to the number of inventory items and the frequency with which these items are withdrawn by the user and replaced with new supplies. The goal of inventory stores management then becomes staying current with the movement of the inventory items and keeping a record of the movement.

Three areas of management become important in achieving these goals — stores, physical inventory, and records and procedures. The concept of stores pertains to the actual management of materials within the organization. Physical inventory becomes necessary because, no matter how carefully records are maintained and procedures are followed, the actual level of inventories is never certain until they are physically counted and accounted for. Records and procedures are important because they help managers keep up with the movement of the inventory and they leave a paper trail.

Stores

There are two major types of stores — closed stores and open stores. *Closed stores* refers to a centralized area where materials are kept in a closed environment. *Open stores*, in contrast, refers to many decentralized areas where materials are kept close to the point of use. Control is the focus in the case of closed stores, and easy access is the focus in the case of open stores.

In a closed stores system, every time material is received or released, it is counted and recorded. Nothing is transacted without the proper paperwork. Centrally controlling stores in this way tends to require more resources. Therefore, its costs must be balanced by consolidating resources, offering better service to users, and reducing the loss of materials. One successful example comes from MDP Products, an outdoor equipment manufacturer located in Willard, Ohio. It consolidated its stores into one location and was able to reduce costs (for example, higher rate of space utilization), better control its inventories, and improve service.[7] Another firm consolidated its storage areas to cut costs. Gulf States Paper Corp., a manufacturer of the paperboard used in food cartons and posterboards, realized that its storage system, which was scattered through several buildings, was ineffective in managing costs and maintaining service, so the corporation consolidated all stores into one location.[8] The results improved inventory control and accuracy and decreased the time needed to retrieve stored items.

However, even in these successful cases, the organizations find themselves keeping bulky or oversized inventories in open areas. So, keeping inventories in an open area is an alternate option for storage. The major characteristic of open stores is that they are scattered throughout the company in open areas where workers may access and retrieve materials at their convenience. Often, open stores include not only bulky or oversized items but also smaller items, such as assembly parts or copy paper. The advantage of this storage system is that the inventories are kept close to the point where the material will be used. Typically, decentralized stores require less space and a lesser degree of handling compared to the closed, centralized stores. However, a higher number of stores personnel are needed for open stores.

Physical Inventories

The goal of a physical inventory count is to confirm the level of inventory shown on the record by physically counting the materials in storage. There are two different strategies that managers have used to take physical inventories. The first strategy requires a complete shutdown of the plant. During this time, teams of inventory counters will account for all materials in closed stores and on the shop floor. Once the inventory has been counted and the discrepancies reconciled, plant operations can resume.

A cycle count (or continuous inventory) represents a second strategy. This strategy does not cause the large inconvenience and disruption that a complete shutdown does to production. For this system, a team of inventory counters counts a group of inventory items at a regular time period and updates the inventory records on an ongoing basis.

Records and Procedures

The basic record forms used to communicate inventory information within an organization include the following:

- Purchase requisitions are issued by inventory control personnel to place orders for new quantities of materials from suppliers.
- Shop orders are used by inventory control personnel when requesting new quantities of materials from an internal shop.
- Receiving reports include records of new materials that have arrived and gone through the receiving process.
- Stores requisitions are prepared by the production supervisor or the line foreman to release the inventories from stores to the shop floor.
- Inspection reports are used to review the quality of either materials from a supplier or parts and subassemblies made by the internal shop.

These forms are key sources of information regarding inventory control. Although the names of such forms may vary, it is important to understand the functions that the forms serve.

The simplest way to maintain the flow of inventory going in and out of stores is to use either ledgers or cards. Each entry can be made by hand or typed, and the forms can be updated manually. Basic data can be input into computers and can be analyzed and compiled for reports. However, bar codes and scanners are facilitating the instantaneous transfer of point-of-transaction information.

In grocery stores and department stores, point-of-sale information is automatically compiled and transferred to warehouses and manufacturers, and it works as the "pull" signal for replenishment. Much of the information transfer procedures can be executed through the Internet-based EDI systems. For instance, Oregon Child Nutrition Coalition, a food co-op that serves 81 private and public schools in Oregon, has adopted an e-commerce strategy and installed Internet-based software to allow the demand to efficiently pull its procurement activities.[9] According to Janet Beer, the district's food service director, "The program has simplified procurement processes and reduced inventory costs."

Inventory Valuation

In contrast to the physical nature of inventory management, the financial nature of inventory management is more subjective, and changes would depend on the valuation procedure adopted by the organization. Consequently, inventory valuation procedures focus on the problem of pricing inventories and have virtually no association with the physical materials themselves. These procedures seek to accomplish an accurate costing of a production operation and are not motivated by the profit making. Ultimately, if all inventory was sold or otherwise disposed of, such procedures would balance inventory out to zero. There are four principal procedures for calculating inventory values.

Under the procedure of *first-in, first-out* (FIFO), the value of the inventory that has been in storage the longest time is applied to the value of goods sold. Thus, when releasing materials, the oldest price into inventory is the first price out of the inventory. In an inflationary economic environment, FIFO implies that the materials being sold now were purchased at lower prices than would be paid today.

With the alternative, *last-in, first-out* (LIFO), the value of the inventory that has been in storage the shortest time is applied to the value of goods sold. When releasing materials, the newest lot is issued first, then the next, and so on. In an inflationary environment, LIFO implies that the materials being sold now came in at higher prices than the materials that remain in inventory. Therefore, LIFO procedures lead to less taxable income in an inflationary environment, whereas FIFO procedures lead to less taxable income in a deflationary environment. To prevent organizations from arbitrarily creating favorable tax positions, the Internal Revenue Service requires organizations to obtain permission before they switch from one inventory valuation procedure to another.

The third procedure is called *average value*. In this case, value is estimated based on a moving average of the materials as new items come into storage. It is not based on which items came in or out first; the average cost changes as new shipments are received.

The fourth procedure relies on *standard costs* to compute the inventory value. Regardless of the prices paid, the materials are charged against the predetermined standard costs for all such items. The standard is usually established based on replacement costs or an average of past prices. Differences between standard costs and actual prices paid must be adjusted for tax purposes.

Inventory Performance

As discussed earlier in this chapter, inventories serve useful purposes, but both money and personnel are needed to control them. Therefore, devising a system to measure inventory performance becomes imperative. Managers typically measure inventory performance in three ways — average inventory value, weeks of supply, and inventory turnover.

Average Inventory Value

Inventories are considered to be assets in an organization's financial statements; however, until they are transformed into a product and lead to a sale, they do not contribute to income. So, the total value of inventory tells managers about how much of an organization's assets are tied up in inventory. The total average inventory value (AIV) is the sum of the values of all items in storage:

AIV =   (Average Inventory Level of Item 1)(Value of Item 1) +
(Average Inventory Level of Item 2)(Value of Item 2) +
(Average Inventory Level of Item 3)(Value of Item 3) +
(Average Inventory Level of Item 4)(Value of Item 4) + . . .

Suppose there are five items in inventory and their average levels and values are shown in the following:

Item	Average Inventory Level	Value Per Item ($)
1	500	0.50
2	250	1.50
3	400	0.75
4	1,000	0.80
5	800	1.25

Then, the total average inventory value is shown as:

$$AIV = (500)(0.50) + (250)(1.50) + (400)(0.75) + (1,000)(0.80) + (800)(1.25) = 250 + 375 + 300 + 800 + 1,000 = \$2,725$$

In general, organizations maintain about 15 to 40 percent of their assets in inventory. For retailers, this figure typically hovers around 75 percent. Ultimately, managers must decide the desired level of AIV for their organizations through subjective judgment based on the desired level of service or the inherent level of uncertainty in their lines of business.

Weeks of Supply

Weeks of supply is computed by dividing the total average inventory value by the value of products sold during one week. The equation to compute the weeks of supply is:

$$\text{Weeks of Supply} = AIV / (\text{Value of Products Sold in One Week})$$

The numerator includes the value of all types of inventory, whereas the denominator includes only the value of products or finished goods sold without the markup. This measure offers the equivalent number of weeks of inventory on hand, based on the value of the products sold. A similar measure, "days of supply," can be computed at the daily level by dividing AIV by the value of products sold in one day.

Inventory Turnover

Inventory turnover is the most common measure for inventory performance. It is the ratio of the value of the products sold (without the sales markup) to the average investment in inventory for the same time period:

$$\text{Inventory Turnover} = (\text{Value of Products Sold in a Time Period}) / AIV$$

The time period can be weeks or months, but organizations most commonly use inventory turnover as an annual measure. The implication is that the higher the inventory turnover, the lower the investment in inventory and the lower the cost of managing inventory. Also, high inventory turnover implies shorter cycle time and thus more operational flexibility and adaptability.

Inventory Control and PSM's Role

Purchasing and supply management (PSM) plays the central role in managing the flow of goods to the organization from the supplier. Purchasing managers traditionally have been in charge of the inventory of raw materials (including purchased parts) and supplies — the procurement activities that occur between a buying organization and a supplier. However, with the emergence of JIT and JIT II, as well as mass customization strategies, the purchasing department's role in inventory control has been expanded beyond the organizational interface. PSM managers now become involved in both the supplier's operation and the buying organization's internal operation. They evaluate the supplier's operations through programs such as supplier certification, and they become part of their own organization's internal operations through programs such as consignment buying. Nonetheless, the goals of purchasing are always the same — to procure the materials in the right quantity and quality, to ensure delivery from the right source at the right place and time, and to pay the right price.

In a supplier certification program, the purchasing department takes the lead role in working with suppliers to get them to improve their processes, to conduct the necessary quality tests, and to include the results of the tests with shipments. As long as the supplier performs the quality tests as agreed, and these tests are verified by the purchasing department, the buying organization can forgo incoming inspections and save on personnel, because the material has already been checked for quality. This type of program can have a profound impact on the level of inventory that the buying organization must invest in. With a working supplier certification program, the buying organization could invest in considerably less inventory.

Such certification programs are also a prerequisite for any type of JIT program. Without them, JIT would not be possible because of the time needed for the buying organization to conduct inspections. Once the supplier can be trusted to deliver the right materials at the right quality, the purchasing managers should work with both internal operations and suppliers to stabilize the production flow and reduce lot sizes and transportation costs. Then, the situation is ripe for JIT — for the buying organization to receive the materials in smaller quantities and at more frequent intervals. However, for JIT to work, the purchasing department must establish a long-term, cooperative relationship with the supplier. Then, the buying organization can enjoy the necessary inflow of materials smoothly feeding into production with minimal inventory and inspection costs.

When JIT is not an option because of the type of materials purchased (for example, rolled steel) or type of production process (for example, job shop processes with high setup costs), the buyer may shift the responsibility of storing incoming materials to the supply end. First, suppliers are more familiar with their finished goods (that is, raw materials for the buyer) and are better qualified to manage their particular type of material. Second, because the number of different types of inventories is typically higher at the raw materials end than at the finished goods end, the supplier can be more proficient at storing its finished goods than the buyer would be. Finally, because it may be supplying the same material to more than one buyer, the supplier can gain greater economies of scale in terms of stores management. Also, the supplier could maintain a lower overall level of safety stock than would be necessary for separate buying organizations.

For example, many steel mill customers, such as John Deere, have been transferring the responsibility of keeping steel inventories to the steel manufacturers. They have requested that steel mills deliver steel JIT (that is, deliveries in smaller lots arriving more frequently). Therefore, steel mills have been working toward successfully making JIT deliveries while reducing their inventories. By implementing a software package developed by I2 Technologies, U.S. Steel, Armco, and Wheeling-Pittsburgh have tapped into their customers' order forecasts.[10] The results have been more on-time deliveries and a reduction of finished goods inventory.

In cases where a buyer purchases a large amount of materials from one supplier, that supplier may be asked to maintain a store on the buying organization's premises and to manage the store based on consignment. Internal users would go to the store as the need arises, and the buying organization would be billed at the end of a time period (for example, a month). The purchasing department typically makes initial arrangements with the supplier and then continues to work with both the suppliers and operations personnel to make sure the suppliers store the right type of materials at the right quantity, based on demand patterns and leadtime.

Key Points

1. The key classifications of inventory are raw materials, work-in-process goods, finished goods, and supplies.
2. The demand for one item does not affect the demand of another item in an independent demand environment. However, the demand for one item triggers the demand of other items in a dependent demand environment.
3. In a fixed order quantity (FOQ) system, the order quantities remain the same, while the time between orders varies. However, in a fixed time period (FTP) system, the periods between orders remain constant, while the inventory positions vary each time an order is placed.
4. The MRP system includes three types of inputs — master production schedule, inventory information, and BOM. It produces a report that informs managers about what to make, how much to make, and when to make it.
5. Inventory turnover is the most common measure for inventory performance. It is the ratio of the value of the products sold to the average investment in inventory for the same time period.

Questions for Review

1. How does carrying inventory facilitate the operation of an organization? How does it adversely affect the operation of an organization?
2. What does the EOQ model try to minimize? What are the two types of cost EOQ tries to optimize?
3. Explain the logic behind ABC analysis.
4. What are the advantages and disadvantages of having closed stores and/or open stores?
5. During an inflationary period, which inventory valuation procedure between first-in, first-out (FIFO) and last-in, first-out

(LIFO) creates a more favorable tax position? Can an organization change the valuation procedure to improve its tax position depending on the economic conditions?

6. How does PSM contribute to inventory control? How has PSM's role in inventory control changed over time and why?

For Additional Information

Chase, R.B., N.J. Aquilano, and F.R. Jacobs. *Production and Operations Management: Manufacturing and Services*, Irwin McGraw-Hill, New York, NY, 1998, pp. 625-677.

Engardio, P. "Souping Up the Supply Chain," *Business Week*, August 24, 1998, pp. 110-112.

Harrington, L. "If Your Partner's a Gorilla…," *Industry Week*, April 5, 1999, pp. 28-35.

Hausman, E., and W. Hersch. "Improved Ordering — Resellers Seek Systems to Track Pricing and Availability from a Single Interface," *Information Week*, March 2, 1998.

Karmarkar, U. "Getting Control of Just-In-Time," *Harvard Business Review*, September/October 1989, pp. 122-131.

Kurtz, M., L. Bongiorno, K. Naughton, G. DeGeorge, and S. Anderson. "Reinventing the Store," *Business Week*, November 27, 1995, pp. 84-86.

Nation's Restaurant News. "Cleaning Up with OSCAR: New Computerized POS Management System Will Cut Costs, Boost Efficiency," August 1996, p. 72.

Parks, L. "Co-Managed Inventory is Focus of Vendor/Retailer Pilot," *Drug Store News*, January 1999, p. 71.

Parks, L. "CPFR Programs Facilitate Inventory Management," *Drug Store News*, February 1999, p. 27.

Sheridan, J. "Managing the Chain," *Industry Week*, September 6, 1999, pp. 50-55.

Souhrada, L. "The Yin and Yang: OR and Materials," *Materials Management in Health Care*, March 1999, pp. 18-20.

Endnotes

1. Ramstad, E. "Koss CEO Gambles on Inventory Buildup," *The Wall Street Journal*, March 15, 1999.
2. Suzaki, K. *The New Manufacturing Challenge: Techniques for Continuous Improvement*, Free Press, New York, NY, 1987.
3. Amato-McCoy, D. "Five Ahold Divisions Will Integrate Unit Operations," *Supermarket News*, March 29, p. 19.
4. Kaydo, C. "Helping Customers Buy On-Line," *Sales & Marketing Management*, July 1999, p. 90.
5. *PM Network*. "Streamlined Information Management Increases Production," April 1999, p. 7.
6. Moad, J. "R/3: Little Material Gain for Applied," *PC Week*, May 20, 1996, p. 1.
7. *Materials Handling Engineering*. "Very Narrow Aisle Trucks Solve Storage Problem," June 1999, p. 98.
8. *Materials Handling Engineering*. "Cost-Cutting Ideas: Storage System Saves Time, Money," August 1999, p. 117.
9. Rubinstein, E. "Oregon Co-op Uses Internet System to Traverse the E-Commerce Trail," *Nation's Restaurant News*, July 5, 1999, p. 49.
10. Woker, C. "Shrinking the JIT Window," *New Steel*, May 1999, pp. 50-53.

CHAPTER 4

INVENTORY STRATEGIES AND DISPOSAL

How do inventory decisions affect the customer? How do they affect the organization's profits? What are the underlying issues regarding disposal of materials, and how do these issues have an impact on the bottomline?

Chapter Objectives

- To consider the financial impact of inventory
- To discuss how inventory management is related both to operational capacity and to sales and marketing
- To review reasons for disposing of surplus or obsolete materials and equipment and purchasing and supply management's responsibility in this endeavor
- To list categories of goods that would be subject to disposal and to identify disposal methods

Inventory's Dual Role

As discussed in the previous chapter, inventory plays a dual role. The proper amount of inventory is necessary to keep the internal operations running smoothly and to help firms overcome uncertainties inherent in the business world. At the same time, keeping inventory requires an investment and assumes risks involved with any type of investment decision.

These issues are discussed in this chapter in terms of the impact inventory has on the organization's bottomline. Also discussed is the management of inventories that have served their purposes and are now obsolete. Disposing of these materials has an impact not only on the organization's profit but also on society at large. Therefore, the issue of surplus management and inventory disposal is also covered.

How are Inventories Related to the Bottomline?

An organization typically uses three measures as indicators of the corporate bottomline — net profit, return on investment, and cash flow. The cost of inventory plays a key role in all three of these measures. The net profit is an absolute measure in dollars, whereas return on investment is a relative measure based on money invested to generate profits. Cash flow is a measure of how well an organization can pay its bills. In corporate accounting, a low level of raw materials inventory typically translates into a higher net profit. Also, inventories are considered to be assets, which affect the calculations of asset turnover and return on investment. However, if inventories are tied up in production operations and in warehouses, this may affect the organization's ability to pay its bills. Thus, the measure of cash flow becomes another important indicator of the corporate bottomline.

An alternate way to consider the impact inventories have on an organization's bottomline derives from Goldratt's theory of constraints.[1] Goldratt determined that the goal of a company is to make money, and in order to make money the company must increase throughput and decrease inventory and operating expenses. He defined *throughput* as the rate at which a company generates money through sales, *inventory* as the amount of money the company has invested in purchased items that will be sold in the market, and *operating expenses* as the money the company spends to transform inventory to throughput. Thus, the bottomline refers to the difference between throughput and the combination of inventory and operating expenses during a specific time period. For instance, when a plant operates all of its production equipment at maximum capacity, it will invariably accumulate inventory. On paper, the productivity of this plant may appear high, because the machines are running all the time (that is, high utilization rate). However, given the same level of sales, the plant's bottomline is now in a poorer condition than it would have been if all equipment had been running in a more balanced manner, because the operating expenses and the money tied up in inventory have increased.

Costs of Inventory

Inventories help managers deal with uncertainties in order to meet both external customer demand and internal user demand. However, if an organization has inventory, it also incurs costs. The major areas of inventories considered here are item costs, ordering costs, holding costs, and stockout costs.

Item Costs

Item costs are incurred from two sources. The first cost is incurred when an item is purchased from a supplier. It refers to the purchase price of an item, including any extra direct costs associated with bringing it to the buying organization (that is, transportation, duties, and insurance costs). The other cost is incurred when goods are manufactured in-house, which typically includes the costs of direct labor, raw materials, and overhead. The purchasing department would have cost information on items purchased from a supplier, and the accounting department would have cost information on items manufactured in-house. If an organization is service-oriented (for example, a bookstore or the local Department of Motor Vehicles), it would typically incur only the first type of item cost. However, manufacturing companies (for example, a household appliance manufacturer or a local restaurant) may incur both types of item costs.

Ordering Costs

Every time an organization places an order, either externally with a supplier or internally with the in-house factory, it entails transaction activities (for example, filling out forms, making telephone calls, and so on), which incur costs. One important characteristic of ordering costs is that the cost is incurred by the frequency of ordering but not by the quantity in each order. For example, if the size of the order is 10, as opposed to 1,000, the total item costs may vary, but the costs incurred in transacting one particular order remain the same. For instance, if the procurement staff at an elementary school orders new chairs out of a catalog, it takes about the same amount of time on the phone or on the computer to place the order and requires the same type of documents to be processed (for example, order notification, receiving invoice, and so on), whether the size of the order is 10 or 1,000 chairs.

If the nature of the order is such that it cannot be clearly specified or it is not available in a catalog, the purchaser may issue requests for quotation (RFQ) or requests for proposal (RFP). The purchaser will then evaluate responses, visit supplier plants, select the right supplier, and negotiate a contract. All of these activities are part of the ordering cost. In the case of an item manufactured in-house, there are production control costs, which vary according to the number of orders rather than the size of orders. Also included are costs associated with setting up a machine for the new order. Therefore, when a make or buy decision is being considered, it makes sense to analyze the total ordering cost, which accounts for not only the ordering costs for interfacing with an external organization, but also the ordering costs incurred internally when an order is manufactured in-house.

Holding Costs

These costs are incurred by an organization for carrying inventory, that is, keeping stock on hand. By investing in inventory stock, an organization assumes the cost of not having invested that money elsewhere — this cost is often referred to as *opportunity cost*. Additionally, an organization must pay for storage space, its upkeep, and the handling of the inventory. The organization must pay taxes for its inventory as an asset, insurance on this asset, and other risk costs such as obsolescence, which result from design changes, changes in market demand, damage during handling, pilferage of inventory, and deterioration of inventory (for example, from rotting or rusting).

Stockout Costs

A stockout occurs when the demand exceeds forecast. This situation is potentially very expensive for the organization because it can lead to the loss of customer confidence or eventually to the loss of the sale. Customers, at first, may be willing to wait, in which case the organization can regard the customers' orders as back orders, but as customers lose confidence in the organization's ability to meet due dates, they must consider how to deal with this added uncertainty. Some customers may consider increasing their level of safety stock. Eventually, there may come a point when the customers' cost of working with this organization is too high, resulting in the justification to look for alternate suppliers.

Capacity Issues

The demand for a given item may vary. At one time, the demand may exceed capacity, and at another time, the demand may be well below capacity. There are many ways to react to changes in demand, including having employees work overtime or reducing their work hours; hiring extra workers or laying off workers; and renting or loaning equipment. However, these options are often quite difficult, given labor management contracts and other ethical, legal, and organizational issues. For instance, an airline company cannot lay off its pilots or mechanics just because the consumer demand for a particular route has gone down. Therefore, many airlines try to level out the demand by taking a conservative stance on the number of flights offered and then overbooking the available seats. A potential drawback to this approach, of course, is unhappy customers who had reserved seats but could not get on the plane. In much the same way, a manufacturing company can try to level its production so that the capacity is used at a consistent level and, as a result, the company would produce extra products during off periods to meet increased demand during peak periods. One drawback to this approach is that the company must incur the holding costs for this inventory between off and peak periods.

It is also important to consider balancing the capacity across a series of dependent operations within an organization. As a general rule, capacity should increase as the operation moves from upstream to downstream. For instance, in both manufacturing and services, a series of dependent operations are brought together to offer value to the customer. Variability is inherent in each operation. For example, the rate of service by an employee varies, and the dimensions of widgets produced at one workstation also vary. Furthermore, as the process moves from one dependent operation to the next, the variabilities add up. This means that the downstream operation should have a higher capacity to absorb the accumulated variability resulting from upstream operations. This is why in a service context, such as a dentist's office or a school cafeteria, customers are placed in a queue when they get to the end of the dependent operations. For example, patients wait for the dentist to look things over after their teeth have been cleaned by a dental hygienist, or customers wait to pay a cashier after picking up their meals in a cafeteria. In these types of service contexts, the customer absorbs the brunt of the accumulated variability (for example, by waiting in line). However, in manufacturing, the manufacturer has to bear the cost of variability (such as idling workers or missed deadlines). This is why, according to Goldratt, it is important to focus on balancing the flow of operations, even if it means building excess capacity in different parts of the factory. If it is not possible to add additional capacity at downstream operations, the only other way to manage the flow is to accumulate the work-in-process inventories to decouple the operations that have varied demand levels imposed on them.

Customer Service

The primary objectives of inventory management are to ensure a high level of customer service and to minimize the organization's investment in inventory. These two, seemingly conflicting, objectives have forced inventory managers to look for the balance between the costs and benefits of maintaining inventory. As such, the organization must define the level of customer service and the amount of stock that it is willing to tolerate.

It is important to articulate who the customers are. Are they internal or external? Because the previous chapter detailed how inventory management is related to serving internal users, this chapter focuses on external customer service. Also, it is important to remember that the definition of "customers" can be expanded beyond the immediate external customer to include the general public. The general public is affected by the products that have outlived their usefulness. For one, the public often pays for the disposal of these products and has to live with the disposed materials. In other words, when considering the topic of customer service, the issue of disposal and related social responsibility considerations are inescapable.

Nature of Customer Service

Because outstanding customer service is ultimately the goal of all organizations in the supply chain, this section introduces a definition of customer service in the supply chain context. Then, elements of customer service at the organizational level will be considered.

La Londe, Cooper, and Noordewier[2] define customer service as "a process for providing significant value-added benefits to [the] supply chain in a cost-effective way." What does this mean? Customer service is a process. It entails a series of dependent operations. In addition, the process must offer value to all organizations in the supply chain, because one organization's supplier is another organization's customer. Finally, an inventory manager needs to balance the cost of delivering the service to the customer and the cost of the investment required to hold inventory. Thus, all customer service activities take place continuously for each firm in the supply chain (pre-transaction, transaction, and post-transaction). Knowledge of customer service elements throughout the different stages of the transaction is essential.

The results of a customer service survey sponsored by the National Council of Physical Distribution Management showed that different elements of customer service existed during the different stages of a transaction.[3] Some notable *pre-transaction* elements include contextual factors, such as policy statements, organizational structure, and system flexibility. These elements cannot be attained in a short period of time; they must be cultivated. For instance, an insurance company may institute a policy on the number of days it takes to process a new application and create an infrastructure to comply with this new policy. *Transaction* elements include stockout levels, the ability to quickly clear back orders, quick order cycles, order convenience, and product substitution. These elements help to facilitate the actual transaction, and at this point, the inventory manager must deal with the issue of short-term costs versus required service levels. For example, a restaurant manager grapples constantly with the freshness of the food served and the preparation cycle time as a function of the level of perishable goods inventories. Customer service, of course, does not end with the transaction. *Post-transaction* elements include warranties, repairs, product tracking, and customer complaints. Even though such services take place after the sale, they must be planned for prior to the transaction.

In the National Council of Physical Distribution Management survey, La Londe and Zinszer also found that product availability (having inventory to consistently satisfy customer requirements) and order cycle time (the time between order placement and order fulfillment) were key issues for customers.

Availability

Availability corresponds with the capacity to have inventory available when it is requested by the customer. In this context, two sources determine the level of inventory — anticipation of customer demand and the desire to cover for inaccuracies in this anticipation. The former is driven by sales forecasts and customer orders — it is typically referred to as the *base stock*. The latter is referred to as *safety stock*, and it is driven by a safety stock policy. Safety stock exists to cover the uncertainties that exist in both forecasting and the replenishment process. The higher the uncertainty, the higher the safety stock level.

Availability is typically measured in three ways — stockout frequency, fill rate, and orders shipped complete. A stockout refers to when demand exceeds supply. Therefore, *stockout frequency* means the frequency of how often this occurs. *Fill rate* describes the degree of severity of stockouts. For instance, if the order is for 100 products but only 90 products are available for shipment, the fill rate is said to be 90 percent. Organizations typically measure fill rates over a period of time and across different customers to obtain a useful measure of availability. *Orders shipped* complete is the most stringent measure of the three. It measures how many times that customer orders were shipped complete; therefore, it excludes all stockouts and partial shipments.

Order Cycle Time

Order cycle time refers to how quickly a customer's order is processed, shipped, and delivered. Of course, product availability plays a significant role in reaching a satisfactory order cycle time.

However, there are other inventory management activities to consider if satisfactory order cycle time is to be accomplished.

The order cycle begins with the receipt of an order and ends with the delivery of the product to the customer. The stages in the cycle are order processing, order picking, order packing, and order delivery. If an order requires in-house manufacturing, the order cycle includes production time. In general, maintaining high product availability and communicating within the organization regarding the status of the required parts and products become instrumental in accomplishing a satisfactory total order cycle time.

Inventory Disposal

When inventory has outlived its useful purpose, it will typically be disposed of in some fashion. Management must carefully control the disposal process to reduce cost or increase profits and to be socially responsible.

Economic Reasons for Disposal

When materials and equipment become obsolete, they tie up capital and incur holding costs for the organization. It is in the organization's best interest to dispose of such materials and equipment in an efficient manner and to recover as much of the capital invested as possible. The following are some key reasons behind disposal.

Investment Recovery – Recovering costs from surplus and obsolete goods has a direct impact on the total cost of production. Because the total cost of production refers to the difference between the total cost of goods sold and the dollars recovered, the higher the recovered value, the lower the total cost of production. Recovery or salvage is a significant area for management involvement in many organizations. For example, a study on investment recovery, sponsored by the CAPS Research (CAPS), collected information from a sample of 65 leading investment departments. In 1997, these departments' average gross revenue was more than $11 million, and the average benefit provided by each professional (exempt) investment recovery was $3.4 million.

Space Management – Surplus and obsolete goods take up storage space. An opportunity cost is associated with storing these goods, because the storage space is not being used for productive purposes. Also, if the organization is renting the space, the rent paid to store obsolete materials makes little economic sense.

Economic Obsolescence – A piece of equipment may become economically obsolete, even while it is still fully functioning. Economic obsolescence of equipment occurs when an organization concludes that the adoption of new technology makes more economic sense, thus rendering its existing technologies obsolete. For instance, a printing company may use separate printing and binding machines. However, when equipment is developed to handle both printing and binding in one process, the company may decide to render existing printing and binding equipment obsolete and adopt the new technology.

Legal Issues for Disposal

The health and safety of workers was addressed in the Federal Occupational Safety and Health Act (OSHA), which was passed in 1970. The purpose of OSHA is "to assure so far as possible every working man and woman in the nation safe and healthful working conditions and to preserve our human resources." The U.S. Department of Labor has worked with the states to establish guidelines to protect workers from handling and processing harmful and unsafe materials. Significant fines have been imposed on organizations for willful violation of the Act. Because the domain of PSM professionals includes the management of materials, they must remain abreast of the legal contexts surrounding the disposal of materials.

OSHA regulates industries and organizations through the implementation of Material Safety Data Sheets (MSDS) — the information available to workers about hazardous materials and other health hazards. The Act also requires that workers receive training regarding the nature of these materials and hazards and the best ways to handle them.

The Resource Conservation and Recovery Act (RCRA), which was passed in 1976, is considered the cornerstone law on industrial waste control. The Act identifies industrial wastes that are harmful and dangerous to human health and welfare, and it regulates all aspects of managing these wastes from initial generation to final disposal.

Two Acts give the Environmental Protection Agency the authority to regulate hazardous waste sites and to recover costs from organizations that are responsible for damage — the Comprehensive Environmental Response, Compensation, and Liability Act of 1980, coupled with the Superfund Amendments and the Reauthorization Act (Superfund or SARA). Hazardous waste is defined as a "toxic, ignitable, corrosive, or dangerously reactive substance." In essence, Superfund controls the hazardous waste released into the environment and its proper disposal.

In 1990, Congress passed the Hazardous Materials Transportation Uniform Safety Act. This is considered to be the primary law concerning the transportation of hazardous materials. It regulates hazardous materials classification, equipment design, and packaging and handling. It takes precedence over local and state regulations on similar issues concerning the environment.

Virtually all organizations generate some type of hazardous waste. In the early 1990s, U.S. organizations produced more than 200 million tons of hazardous waste each year. Managers in charge of the hazardous wastes (often purchasing managers) must communicate and disclose what these wastes are to all concerned parties (for example, employees, transportation companies, customers, and the general public). Then the managers must educate employees regarding how best to work with these wastes. Also, managers should continuously examine employees for any ill effects resulting from exposure to such materials. The basic rule is that whoever generates the hazardous material should be responsible for it from "cradle to grave" (that is, from its generation to its ultimate disposal).

Social Responsibility Regarding Disposal Management

As organizations deplete more and more natural resources, they should become more conscious of the social implications of their actions. In other words, their actions for the disposal of obsolete materials should go beyond economic and legal requirements. Ben and Jerry's is a successful U.S. company that uses two types of managerial control — financial and social. The organization manufactures ice cream, which produces byproducts that must be disposed of. Because social responsibility is one of this organization's control mechanisms, its management sometimes invests in a new business venture in order to create an environmentally sound way of disposing of the byproducts it produces. At one point, Ben and Jerry's ventured into a hog-farming business because it discovered that hogs thrive on ice cream byproducts. Ben and Jerry's continues to investigate sound, environmentally friendly ways to dispose of its wastes.

It is important for organizations to proactively create and implement policies regarding waste disposal. Ellram and Birou pointed out several proactive measures involving purchasing personnel.[4] They suggested that purchasing become involved early in the product development stage so it can suggest environmentally friendly raw materials and parts. For instance, IBM decided to design its plastic computer parts without metal inserts so that the plastic can be more easily recycled, and Kodak, by design, reuses more than 85 percent of materials for making its single-use cameras.[5]

An organization can apply for "green certification" programs. For example, the European Community (EC) has devised the BS7750 program, which provides a framework to create proactive goals regarding environmental standards. General Motors (GM) and Ford soon will require all of their suppliers to comply with the international environmental standards on air, water, chemicals, and recycling set by the International Organization for Standardization (ISO) — GM by the end of 2002 and Ford by 2003.[6] Hewlett-Packard also implemented an environmentally conscious procurement policy that has evaluated its suppliers for environmental friendliness since 1993.[7]

However, choosing between environmentally friendly suppliers versus less environmentally friendly suppliers often presents a dilemma for many organizations when the costs of being environmentally friendly are excessive. Even the most ardent, environmentally oriented managers can retreat from their beliefs when the organization's profit line is at stake. For instance, Duncan Berry, who had been a dedicated environmentalist, grappled with such a dilemma and ended up making a profit-oriented choice.[8] Even after discovering that the raw materials his company was using (cotton) came from an industry that released harmful chemicals into farmlands, which eventually got into food and cattle feed, he could not justify the less profitable route of selecting the more expensive, but organically produced, cotton. Torn between managerial issues and his personal beliefs regarding the environment, he eventually resigned from a board that oversees an environmental sanctuary off the coast of Seattle. This example illustrates the tension between social responsibility and the corporate bottomline and how the answer to this issue may not always be clear.

PSM's Responsibility for Disposal

Purchasing and supply management plays a significant role in the disposal of surplus materials. According to a CAPS report on purchasing's organizational roles and responsibilities, the majority of the firms surveyed (63 percent) responded that the purchasing department was responsible for the disposal and recovery of scrap and surplus goods.[9] Among all the non-purchasing activities listed (including materials planning, stores/warehousing, and inventory control), inventory recovery of scrap and surplus materials was the most frequently listed area of purchasing.

Purchasing professionals typically have comprehensive knowledge about price trends. In general, prices of surplus goods are more volatile than prices of regular raw materials, because the influx of surplus materials into the marketplace is less steady. The market for surplus goods is more removed from the final consumer market, so the effects of final market fluctuations are felt more severely. Therefore, someone who has knowledge and understanding concerning price trends needs to manage the disposal of an organization's surplus materials.

Also, purchasing typically has the most up-to-date information regarding the needs of internal users; thus, it is in the best position to channel surplus goods for internal use. When an organization disposes of surplus internally, it does not have to incur transaction costs to deal with external organizations. Therefore, this method is usually the most economic way to dispose of surplus materials.

Even when an organization needs to dispose of the surplus goods externally, the purchasing department is in the best position to facilitate the transaction. Although this is a sales activity, it is appropriate for purchasing personnel because the products that the organization is trying to dispose of are more often raw materials than finished goods. However, if the surplus goods are finished products, it might be best to transfer the responsibility to the sales department.

Often, the purchasing department may find that it has to work with the operations department to prepare surplus materials for sale. Once a buyer for surplus goods is identified and the specifications are stated, operations may need to help purchasing sort the scrap materials. For instance, the buying organization may request that steel and copper scraps should be separated from other metal scraps. They may further request that steel scraps should be separated from copper scraps and that steel scraps and copper scraps should be segregated into different grades. To get the surplus materials into a desired form, operations may even need to engage in a value transformation process. For instance, the buyer for plastic scraps may request that the selling organization shred the scraps into smaller pieces to facilitate its processing procedures once the materials arrive at the plant.

Compared to other departments, such as marketing or operations, purchasing is more familiar with external regulatory restrictions involving the management of surplus disposal. This is especially true when the process involves hazardous materials, as discussed in the preceding section. Furthermore, purchasing needs to be part of product design teams and inform the other team members about the problems associated with packaging, transportation, and disposal of hazardous materials. The purchasing managers should be ready to suggest alternate, nonhazardous materials that can alleviate the cost of handling hazardous materials.

Categories of Disposable Materials

If an organization is trying to dispose of surplus goods in a meaningful way, it needs to establish policies. In order to set up such policies, the organization must first categorize its disposable materials.

Surplus or Obsolete Materials

Surplus materials are created when purchased amounts exceed the required amount in production and when the produced amount exceeds the sales amount. These materials can result from overly optimistic sales forecasts, faltered sales promotions, unexpected market changes, mistakes in production planning, or extensive forward purchases. Surplus materials often can be stored for reuse at a future date, unless they are perishable (for example, agricultural goods or fashion goods with time-sensitive demand).

If, however, a change in design occurs or a present technology is replaced with a new one, there is little possibility that the stored surplus materials will be used at a future date. In such cases, these materials are rendered obsolete and are called *obsolete materials*. For example, if a memory chip is stored for use in the next model, it is a surplus material. However, if, due to a design change, this chip is no longer required, it becomes an obsolete material.

Therefore, the goal of an organization should be to use up or recover the value of its surplus materials before they become obsolete. Some typical strategies are to use surplus materials as a substitute for another material, move them to a location within the organization where they are needed, or sell them to external customers.

Surplus or Obsolete Equipment, Tooling, and Fixtures

Surplus capacity occurs when a production line is slowed down or stopped. This situation often points to having "surplus" equipment. The tooling and fixtures that are used for that equipment may also become surplus goods. However, when new and more technologically sophisticated equipment is purchased as a replacement, the current equipment is said to be "obsolete." The tooling and fixtures for that equipment, unless they can be used for the new equipment or other equipment, are also rendered obsolete.

Often, the point at which surplus equipment becomes obsolete is a managerial decision. It is important to keep in mind that the organization's goal is to dispose of surplus and obsolete goods economically. One organization's surplus and obsolete goods can be useful and appropriate goods for another firm. E-commerce represents a growing way to manage the disposal of these goods.

Scrap

Scrap refers to goods and materials that are no longer useful — they have expended their useful life, or they serve no immediately useful purpose. Scrap includes worn-out equipment, tooling, and fixtures or reusable residues from normal operations. Examples are worn-out stamping machines, dirty engine oil, and skeleton steel sheets, which result from the stamping of parts. Some scrap can be recycled economically. For example, worn-out stamping machines can be taken apart, and some of their parts can be recycled. Both dirty engine oil and skeleton steel sheets can be recycled as well.

Waste

Scrap that results from mistakes in handling or processing is referred to as waste. Because it has gone through a transformation process, waste can't be returned to an original state where it can be useful (that is, recycled). Some materials, even if they can be recycled, are treated as waste when recycling makes no economic sense (for example, no resale value). Further, perishable materials, if not well maintained, can become waste in relatively short time periods. This is why Boeing opted for smaller but more frequent deliveries of perishable materials, such as paints and adhesives, from its suppliers.[10] The new policy has led to "a tremendous waste savings," according to a Boeing manager.

Hazardous Materials (HazMats)

Hazardous materials are materials or substances that can be potentially harmful to human beings. Many organizations consciously evaluate the implications or risks of using toxic materials and hazardous materials that may create landfill or incinerator problems in their products. To this end, Boeing has developed a policy to evaluate the environmental friendliness of the materials its suppliers use and has discouraged them from using hazardous materials.[11]

One definition of hazardous materials comes from the Hazardous Materials Transportation Act of 1974, which states that a hazardous material is "a substance or material in a quantity and form which may pose an unreasonable risk to health and safety or property...." In this sense, many materials or substances that may appear innocuous can become hazardous if they are handled improperly. For example, it is possible for grain elevators to explode when grain dust catches fire.

And, if stacked up too high, even cartons of white paper that can fall on people can become hazardous.

Seven categories are typically used to describe hazardous materials — explosives, compressed gases, flammable liquids, oxidizers, poisons, radioactive materials, and corrosive materials. These materials, if not handled properly, have the potential to endanger people, equipment, other materials, and the environment. As a result, they should be handled with extra caution.

Hazardous materials may need to be put in special packaging and include special warning labels. They may also need to be stored in special areas. For example, warehouses or storage areas for hazardous materials could include special features, such as a dike around the area with the drainage into a holding tank.

In general, as purchasing formulates the strategy for managing hazardous materials, it should begin by identifying such materials and communicating information about them to employees through the completion and disclosure of Material Safety Data Sheets (MSDS), which were discussed earlier in this chapter. Employees have the "right to know" what they are being exposed to, and they must be trained to handle hazardous materials in a safe manner. In addition to training, the organization should implement plans in case of mishandling or exposure to hazardous materials. The disposal of hazardous waste should also be planned out and executed. As discussed previously, the purchasing department is often placed in charge of this activity. Purchasing may contract out all operations involving waste disposal, or it may contract out portions of the operations, such as packaging or transportation.

Disposal of Surplus Materials

In this section, major channels of surplus and obsolete materials disposal are discussed, along with contracting and pricing practices. Also, an overview of disposal procedures is presented, including activities that will result in a profit from the disposal of surplus and obsolete materials.

Channels of Disposal

Use within the Organization – In general, this is the preferred method of disposing of surplus material, because it incurs no transaction costs for dealing with external organizations. For example, returning material to suppliers may reduce its original value by 10 to 20 percent (that is, the supplier will need to cover its restocking cost). If the organization uses dealers and brokers, it may reclaim even less. Therefore, surplus materials can be advertised through an internal computer network or through memos issued by the purchasing department to other departments. Often, metal scraps can be reused within a firm that stamps out small parts, such as small plates and washers. Obsolete machines in one plant can be reused in other plants within the same organization.

Return to Supplier – After "use within the organization," this is typically the next preferred method of disposing of surplus materials. Sometimes, the original item can be returned (for example, books that did not sell or extra sheet steel in its original rolls). In the case of non-ferrous metals, such as copper, scraps can be returned to the supplier, often at a price higher than can be attained on the open market. In fact, some supplier contracts request that the organization return such scraps to them.

"As-Is" Sale to Others – If done correctly, this method can garner a high price, and it is more profitable than turning to dealers and brokers. As-is sales include surplus raw materials that can be used by another firm as raw materials. Equipment sales made directly to other firms will result in a favorable return for the organization. As-is sales are usually conducted through advertisements in trade journals or Internet auction sites.

Sale to Dealers and Brokers – One advantage of turning to dealers and brokers is that they are often willing to purchase a small quantity of materials. They may accumulate or compile materials to facilitate a bulk sale. Also, they usually have extensive information on potential buyers. Dealers typically will sort materials, and sometimes they will engage in simple fabrications. Brokers are intermediaries whose primary job is to locate a buyer for a specific organization's surplus material.

Various Types of Sales Agreements

Variable Price Contract – The price for surplus material is estimated at the time of pickup. It is determined by subtracting a markup for the dealer or broker from a fair market price. The fair market price can be obtained from published sources, such as *Iron Age, Steel, or American Metal Market*. Prices may also be found on Web sites — amm.com (the Web site of *American Metal Market*) or steel.org (the Web site of the American Iron and Steel Institute).

Fixed Price Contract – This price is agreed upon through negotiations between the seller and the buyer. The agreement should include information on price, quantity, delivery, and terms of payment. Cancellation policies and methods of weight determination should also be included.

Term Contracts – Whether the price is variable or fixed, the agreement can cover a period of time (for example, one month or one year). From the seller's perspective, a longer term contract is advantageous because a buyer, such as a dealer, will be obligated to buy the material regardless of market conditions. From the dealer's perspective, if the market for the particular surplus material has taken a downturn (for example, steel companies are not buying the metal scraps), the dealer will need to accumulate this material until the market condition changes.

Commission – Often a broker or a dealer will take surplus materials and sell them either through established market channels or an auction. After the sale, a commission will be paid to the broker or the dealer from the proceeds, and the organization selling the surplus will receive the net profit.

Procedures for Disposal

Segregation – To ensure the maximum gain from a sale, surplus materials should be segregated from one another. For instance, scrap can be segregated by type, alloy, grade, size, and weight. If surplus materials are mixed, the return on sales will be considerably reduced. Therefore, sorting will be required. In general, it is best for the organization to begin segregating when (and where) scrap surplus is created.

Processing – The organization may choose to process surplus materials per buyer specifications before the sale in order to increase the value of the surplus materials. As long as the organization has excess capacity, it can engage in simple cutting, grinding, or bailing. For instance, if an organization (for example, a salvage dealer) sells worn-out tires to a mini-mill to be used as fuel, no processing is required prior to the sale. However, if this organization is selling to an assembler that will use cut pieces of the tires in its assembly process, the value of the material will increase if the organization has the capacity to cut the tires.

Collection and Classifications – Organizations should set up infrastructures internally to collect and classify surplus materials. Specially trained workers and well-defined procedures may be required. Workers should be trained to recognize the grades of scrap, so they can classify the materials and correctly store them. Depending on both the amount of scrap and the level of scrap mixes generated, procedures should inform workers about the frequency of collections and subsequent activities, such as classifying and routing. As volumes, mixes, and frequencies of surplus material change, the written procedures should be updated. Records for collecting and classifying surplus materials must be accurately maintained.

Negotiation or Competitive Bidding – If the buyer of the surplus materials is another organization, a sales agreement is typically reached through negotiation. Often, one organization is willing to give surplus materials, such as unused paint or wooden pallets, to another organization as long as an agreement can be negotiated for freight-on-board (FOB) its factory yard. However, if there are multiple buyers, such as dealers or brokers, either negotiation or competitive bidding can be used. In the case of competitive bidding, several brokers are invited to come to the factory to inspect and bid on the materials (for example, silver, copper, and their alloys or surplus equipment).

Reporting and Accounting – All sales should be approved by the manager of the business unit, whose total operating cost will be affected by the sale of surplus materials. Records of all transactions should be maintained and sent to all departments involved in the transaction (for example, operations, shipping, and accounting). The final weighing or counting should be done by the shipping department, and this information should be sent to the billing department. The billing department will then log the transaction as accounts receivable and process it through the standard procedure for invoicing and receiving payments. However, it is advisable to track such transactions in separate accounts or on a separate line on financial reports, beyond netting them against raw material costs. This information can be useful in establishing future policies for disposal management and improving infrastructure.

Key Points

1. There are four main categories of costs regarding inventory — item costs, ordering costs, holding costs, and stockout costs.
2. Often, the only solution to a temporary capacity-demand mismatch is to keep inventory.
3. Two key managerial issues in customer service are product availability (having inventory to consistently satisfy customer requirements) and order cycle time (the time between order placement and order fulfillment).
4. Although a piece of equipment may still be fully functional, it may become economically obsolete when a firm decides to adopt a new piece of equipment to replace it. The organization would then be motivated to dispose of the obsolete equipment to recover its investment and to save the costs of the space that the equipment occupies.
5. Material Safety Data Sheets (MSDS) contain information about hazardous materials and other health hazards. They must be made available to workers.
6. Disposable goods are categorized as surplus or obsolete materials and surplus or obsolete equipment, tooling, and fixtures. They are also categorized into scraps, which are goods and materials that no longer serve a useful purpose, and wastes, which are scraps that result from mistakes.
7. Employees have the "right to know" what they are being exposed to, and they must be trained to handle hazardous materials in a safe manner.

8. Disposal procedures begin with segregating or sorting the materials and, if desired, applying simple processing to the materials. An infrastructure should be set up within the firm to collect and classify surplus materials. Once a buyer is found and a contract is reached, the transaction is recorded.

Questions for Review

1. How can inventory both help and hurt an organization's operation?
2. Name at least two reasons why surplus disposal is an important area of management.
3. Who ultimately pays for the disposal of obsolete goods? What can firms do to minimize the cost of disposing of these goods?
4. Identify the social, economic, and governmental pressures that require organizations to manage the disposal of their obsolete goods well.
5. Why should the purchasing department be responsible for the disposal of obsolete goods?
6. What are some possible channels of disposal? Which ones are preferred and why?

For Additional Information

Balden, J.A. *Environmental Gore: A Constructive Response to "Earth in Balance,"* Pacific Research Institute for Public Policy, San Francisco, CA, 1994.

Bloom, G.F. and M.S. Motron. "Hazardous Waste is Every Manager's Problem," *Sloan Management Review*, Summer 1991, p. 80.

Goldratt, E.M. and J. Cox. *The Goal*, North River Press, Great Barrington, MA, 1992.

Gore, Jr., A. *Earth in the Balance: Ecology and the Human Spirit*, Houghton Mifflin, Boston, MA, 1992.

Institutional Investor. "Green is Good," September 1996, pp. 27-28.

Journal of Business Strategy. "ISO 14000 as Job 1?" November 1996, p. 6.

Kharbanda, O.P. and E.A. Stallworthy. *Waste Management: Towards a Sustainable Society*, Auburn House, New York, NY, 1990.

Kilgore, C., G. Wagner, M. Muller, and C. Hartless. "You Can Get There from Here," *Materials Management in Health Care*, April 1999, pp. 28-30.

Narasimhan, R. and J.R. Carter. *Environmental Supply Chain Management*, Center for Advanced Purchasing Studies, Tempe, AZ, 1998.

Occupational Hazards. "Intel Signs Cooperative Agreement with EPA," 1997, p. 32.

Parks, L. "CRP Investment Pays Off in Many Ways," *Drug Store News*, February 1, 1999, p. 26.

Endnotes

1. Goldratt, E.M. *General Theory of Constraints*, Abraham Y. Goldratt Institute, New Haven, CT, 1989.
2. La Londe, B.J., M.C. Cooper, and T.G. Noordewier. *Customer Service: A Management Perspective*, The Council of Logistics Management, Oak Brooke, IL. 1988.
3. La Londe, B.J. and P.H. Zinszer. *Customer Service: Meaning and Measurements*, The Council of Logistics Management, Chicago, IL, 1976.
4. Fearon, H.E. and L.M. Birou. *Purchasing for Bottom Line Impact*, Irwin, Chicago, IL, 1995.
5. Gottlieb, D. "'Design for Environment Movement Seeks to Leapfrog Regs," *Purchasing*, March 1999, p. 53.
6. *Wall Street Journal.* "GM, Ford to Make Their Suppliers Meet 'Green' Standards," September 22, 1999, p. B2.
7. *Wall Street Journal*, 1999.
8. Seglin, J.L. "It's Not That Easy Going Green," *Inc.*, May 1999, pp. 29-32.
9. Fearon, H.E. and M.R. Leenders. *Purchasing's Organizational Roles and Responsibilities*, Center for Advanced Purchasing Studies, Tempe, AZ, 1995.
10. Milligan, B. "Boeing's Environmental Programs Start with Suppliers," *Purchasing*, June 1999, pp. 93-94.
11. Milligan, 1999.

CHAPTER 5

What types of value enhancement programs are there? What tactical issues are involved in implementing such programs in organizations? How can purchasing and supply management (PSM) best contribute to the organization's bottomline?

Chapter Objectives

- To define and justify standardization and simplification
- To review various boards for standardization
- To highlight process improvement programs involving PSM
- To discuss cost reduction and avoidance programs
- To review value engineering and value analysis

Value enhancement was discussed in Chapter 1 as an approach that shows managers how to add value to their organizations. Value enhancement also includes a holistic, systems perspective as key in accomplishing these goals. This chapter will focus on more specific approaches a purchaser can use to accomplish value enhancement. Topics to be addressed include simplification and standardization, process improvement programs, cost reduction strategies, and value engineering and analysis.

Simplification and Standardization

Simplification

There are forces that drive an organization to increase the number and types of products or services it brings to the market.

Customers change their minds at the last minute (that is, requirements change), and different customers demand different things (that is, they exhibit different needs). To capture emerging market segments, an organization is often forced to introduce new products and services, in addition to what it already offers. Diversification of products and services is often a requirement for an organization to satisfactorily meet customers' demands.

However, there is a point of diminishing return for such diversification. Overly diversified products and services lead to inefficiencies (for example, high overhead costs), and the organization may incur a loss. It is costly to manufacture and carry products in a variety of sizes, colors, prices, and so on. It becomes necessary to reduce the varieties. This can be accomplished by redesigning the products or services or by simply eliminating many marginal product lines or services. This process is called *simplification*.

One electrical equipment manufacturer discovered that it had increased its number of products from 2,000 to about 10,000 in three short years. New workers had been hired, and the level of overtime had increased by five times. When the managers came to realize what was going on, it actually surprised them. Subsequently, the managers worked with the customers and prioritized their requirements. Some product lines were redesigned, and others were dropped. Workers were reassigned, and the company reduced its product variety to less than 1,000 without losing any significant customers.

Standardization

Standardization is a useful way to simplify products. It begins with the use of standard measurement specifications for a product's type, color, physical dimensions, chemical composition, and so on. The standard specifications facilitate communication among designers, who can work on increasing the product to parts ratio. For instance, when 100 products are created from 1,000 different parts, the product to parts ratio is 0.1. When, on the other hand, the same 100 products are created from 2,000 different parts, the product to parts ratio is 0.05. The first situation is associated with a higher level of standardization compared to the latter situation.

When common parts are used throughout the organization, repeated use of the parts increases. Thus, the organization is more conducive to standardizing work tasks which, in turn, leads to higher productivity. Standardization of parts and tasks is the backbone of Just-In-Time (JIT) systems, because it leads to shorter cycle times and lower inventories. Without standardization, mass customization would not be possible. Mass customization relies on a high product to parts ratio — creating a higher variety of products given limited types of parts and raw materials.[1]

Implications for PSM

Because the purchasing and supply management department plays an integral role in controlling the sources and characteristics of raw materials and parts, it invariably becomes involved in establishing policies and strategies for simplification and standardization. For instance, Ford PSM professionals worked with their suppliers to reduce the complexity of components and to promote the standardization of parts and subsystems.[2] Without simplification and standardization at the incoming stage, it would be difficult and costly to enforce simplification and standardization strategies in latter stages of operations.

For instance, many plastic molders limit their number of plastic resin suppliers, thus simplifying their work procedures and supplier relationships, in order to ensure the consistency of the resin's chemical composition. Receiving resins from different suppliers often changes the color and texture of the finished product, even though the resins are put through an identical molding process. Another example comes from retail clothing businesses. Clothing retailers do not attempt to stock every size that customers require. They stock clothes in standard sizes and alter them to fit customers. Therefore, a purchasing manager for a clothing retailer would order clothing in standard sizes. He or she would work closely with marketing to identify how much product to order in relationship to the standard sizes the manufacturers offer.

Standards Boards

To ensure the efficiency and uniformity of products and to facilitate the selling and purchasing of products, many standard-setting organizations offer guidelines. Some standards are mandatory (for example, those concerning safety issues), but many are voluntary.

The International Organization for Standardization (ISO) defines standards in the following:

> Standards are documented agreements containing technical specifications or other precise criteria to be used consistently as rules, guidelines, or definitions of characteristics, to ensure that materials, products, processes, and services are fit for their purpose.[3]

The ISO also illustrates how standards can make lives simpler and more convenient. For instance, because of standards imposed on phone cards (for example, 0.76 millimeter thickness), the cards can be used around the world. A buyer can purchase a phone card in Korea, where it is manufactured, travel to Germany, and use it there. This section reviews major international and national standard-setting organizations, beginning with the ISO. To the extent that a PSM professional engages in commerce as a buyer, he or she should understand the goals behind these standard boards and should be familiar with their basic activities and the relationships that exist among them.

International Organization for Standardization (ISO)

The ISO is the major international body dedicated to setting standards for organizations engaged in buying and selling across national borders. This nongovernmental organization was established in 1947 because managers from different countries realized that setting standards is the first step to promoting and ensuring the international trade of goods and services.

The name "ISO" is *not* the abbreviation of the International Organization for Standardization. "ISO" is a prefix that means "equal" (that is, same or standard), as in isometric or isomorphism. According to the *American Heritage Dictionary*, isometric means "exhibiting equality in dimensions or measurements," and isomorphism is "similarity of form...or of structure."

The ISO includes members from approximately 130 countries. Membership is given to one representative organization for each country; each member organization represents the standardization of its country in the most comprehensive way. Each member body has three major tasks:

- It is responsible for disseminating information within its country regarding international standardization initiatives.
- It represents its country's views on issues regarding international standardization.
- It offers the financial support of its country for the operation of the ISO.

Member organizations participate fully in voting procedures regarding technical and policy-setting matters. However, the ISO does allow nonvoting members from less developed countries.

The ISO has made many accomplishments, and its work has affected many industries, including automobiles, shipbuilding, telecommunications, information processing, and packaging and distribution logistics. The ISO has set standards for film speed, telephone and bank cards, freight containers, measurement systems, and so on. One special accomplishment is ISO 9000, which provides standards and guidelines for quality management.

ISO 9000 provides a framework for a quality system that is defined by three levels of quality assurance. Each level is reserved for a different type of organization, and it has a specific number associated with it. The levels are listed in the following:

- Level 1 (ISO 9001) applies to organizations that design, develop, produce, install, and service products — for example, original equipment manufacturers (OEMs) that engage in design and the other activities listed (Ford, GE, and so on).
- Level 2 (ISO 9002) applies to organizations that only produce and install products — for example, parts suppliers that engage in make-to-specifications with no internal design capability.
- Level 3 (ISO 9003) applies to organizations that conduct final inspections and the testing of products.

Two other levels, ISO 9000 and ISO 9004, address the underlying elements of a quality management system and provide directions for applying the appropriate ISO level. In particular, ISO 9004 provides guidelines for developing and implementing a quality management system and for subsequent internal auditing.

International Electrotechnical Commission (IEC)

The IEC collaborates with the ISO on standardization in the areas of information technology and telecommunications. Whereas the ISO's scope includes many different industries, the IEC focuses on electrical, electronic, and related technologies.

The IEC was established in 1906, after a resolution was passed at the 1904 International Electrical Congress in St. Louis, Missouri.[4] The International Electrotechnical Commission was charged with promoting international standards in the areas of electronics, magnetics and electromagnetics, electroacoustics, telecommunications, and energy production and distribution. The commission develops standards and frameworks to promote international trade and economically motivated activities. At the same time, it works to ensure the safety and health of individuals as well as to protect the environment. The IEC publishes standards and technical reports, which can serve as references when purchasers are developing international contracts that involve electrical parts and assemblies.

American National Standards Institute (ANSI)

ANSI is the national body that represents the United States in the ISO and IEC. This body promotes the adoption of U.S. standards in international arenas, and it reports to the United States about international standards that could be adopted as national standards.

ANSI was founded in 1918 in the United States by five engineering societies and three governmental agencies.[5] Its goal is to promote and enhance the global competitiveness of U.S. businesses and the quality of life in the United States. It administers standards that have been voluntarily developed and adopted in the United States. It is a private, nonprofit organization whose membership includes more than 1,000 companies; more than 280 professional, trade, educational, consumer, and labor organizations; and more than 80 government agencies.

ANSI facilitates the process through which American National Standards (ANSs) are developed. Although ANSI does not directly develop ANSs, its members work with qualified groups to develop standards. ANSI follows three guiding principles to develop its standards — consensus, due process, and openness. There are currently more than 175 accredited national standards developers and more than 13,000 approved ANSs. These standards address the products a buyer may be involved in purchasing. There are, for example, guidelines for procuring power station equipment, gas turbines, hose assemblies, and even fasteners. Also, there are safety guidelines for products such as power transformers.

The remainder of this section reviews domestic standard-setting organizations in the United States. All of these organizations are ANSI accredited. The procurement guidelines offered in ANSs may be developed by any one of these organizations.

American Society for Testing and Materials (ASTM)

With 33,000 members, ASTM is one of the largest organizations in the world to facilitate the development of voluntary standards.[6] It provides a forum for qualified and interested people to come together and write standards for materials, products, systems, and services. These people are producers, purchasers, consumers, government representatives, and academics.

More than 134 committees develop the information that ASTM publishes — standard test methods, specifications, practices, guides, classifications, and terminology. The committees focus on the following products: degradable polymers; fuels; lubricants; and cleaning agents, solvents, and surfactants.

American Society for Quality (ASQ)

The ASQ was founded in 1946 as the American Society for Quality Control (ASQC), when members from 17 local quality control societies decided to form a professional organization.[7] To many, this was a culminating event for the United States' emerging interest in quality after World War II. This society includes more than 133,600 individual and 1,100 sustaining members. Membership is open to anyone who is interested in quality.

Its mission is to advance "individual and organizational performance excellence worldwide by providing opportunities for learning, quality improvement, and knowledge exchange." The ASQ currently has more than 250 local sections to which members belong. Members also can join any of its 21 divisions and four technical committees. Approximately 200 staff members carry out the directives developed by its Strategic Planning Committee.

The ASQ is responsible for running the standards committees on behalf of ANSI. These standards committees are called QEDS, which describes the four broad technical disciplines they represent — quality management, environmental management, dependability, and statistics. As the secretariat for ANSI's committee on quality assurance, the ASQ provides leadership to build consensus for national and international standards. For instance, ANSI representatives played a key role in developing and revising ISO 9000 standards.

Society of Automotive Engineering (SAE)

The SAE was founded in 1905 in the United States, and it has about 80,000 members from more than 90 countries who share a common interest in self-propelled vehicles and technologies.[8] The SAE incorporates technical information and the expertise used in designing, manufacturing, maintaining, and operating vehicles in any media possible for traveling (that is, land, sea, air, or space). It supports research, the development of standards, and public programs that promote vehicle safety and maintenance.

Its technical committees develop aerospace and automotive engineering standards. The SAE publishes these standards and other technical books and reports. Many new and revised standards are published in three categories — ground vehicle standards (J-Reports), aerospace standards, and aerospace material specifications (AMS). These standards — which function as an agreement on form, fit, and function — provide a common language that different industries and engineers can use to communicate with one another.

American Society of Mechanical Engineers (ASME)

ASME was founded in 1880 in the United States by a diverse group of engineers who included designers, shipbuilders, industrialists, educators, and technical journalists.[9] Since its inception, ASME has been a leader in the development of technical standards. Beginning with a standard for the screw thread, ASME has developed more than 600 codes and standards. It maintains and distributes these codes and standards, which are used around the world for the design, production, and installation of mechanical devices.

Value Engineering and Value Analysis

The standards set by the associations and societies discussed in the preceding section operate at the national, international, or industry level. This section discusses how individual organizations can simplify their products or services through the process of value engineering and analysis and how PSM professionals play an integral role in this process.

The goal behind value engineering (VE) and value analysis (VA) is to maintain the functionality of the parts or subassembly, but to produce it at a reduced cost. According to Dave Nelson, formerly at Honda and now at Deere and Company, VE is referred to as "the art of tinkering with parts and systems during their design stage to improve value."[10] VA can then be defined as tinkering with parts and systems *after* their design to improve value. The difference between VE and VA is timing — VE occurs during the design stage, and VA happens after the design stage and during each continuous cost improvement stage. However, both activities involve design activities, so they are often referred to as being synonymous.[11] Together, they are typically referred to as VA/VE.

Through VA/VE, it becomes possible to use a component to perform the same functions without additional cost. PSM professionals participate in VA/VE activities because of their knowledge regarding the cost of raw materials and parts, as well as their understanding of suppliers' capabilities. PSM professionals are also in the best position to know the industry benchmark cost for a subassembly, and they would inform the designers if the present cost of a subassembly seems excessive.

In an example of VA/VE, an auto maker had been chrome-coating its power steering columns for aesthetic reasons and to prevent them from rusting. However, the auto maker's engineers eventually realized that, because the steering column is placed behind the dashboard, customers do not really look at it. Further, because moisture usually does not reach the steering column, there was little chance of it rusting. The buyers of this part knew it would be simple to eliminate the chrome-coating step. Therefore, this auto maker kept the functionality of the steering column while reducing its manufacturing cost by asking the supplier to eliminate the chrome-coating.

Function and Cost

When managers engage in VA/VE activities, the functionality of a product and the cost of creating that functionality are always in tension. On one hand, an organization could drive itself out of the market if it insisted on delivering the full functionality of a product at all costs — the functionality of the product may be acceptable to the customer, but the cost may not. The same organization, on the other hand, could also lose its market share if it insisted on driving down the cost, while sacrificing many of its product's functionalities. The sacrificed functionalities may be critical to customers. As stated previously, the goal of VA/VE is to keep the functionality uniform but to reduce the cost of delivering it. In this regard, a product can be viewed as "a bundle of functions." When a customer is willing to pay for this bundle, a market is created. When the cost of delivering this bundle is less than that of the competitors, there is more value for the customers, and the market is being captured. Therefore, continued VA/VE can be critical in maintaining market position. For instance, through VA/VE, the costs of manufacturing the Honda Accord and the Toyota Camry were reduced by more than 25 percent during the late 1990s. That reduction enabled Honda to keep the same sticker price while offering a bigger product with more options; Toyota actually reduced the sticker price of its product.

When managers perform VA/VE, they must address the following questions:

- What are the key functionalities of the product that customers require?
- Can any part or subassembly be eliminated without sacrificing these functionalities?
- Can any part or subassembly be simplified without sacrificing these functionalities?
- Is a substitutable raw material, part, or subassembly available at a lower cost without sacrificing these functionalities?

The marketing department would be involved in addressing the first question. However, once that question is answered, marketing takes on an advisory role. To address the other three questions, the purchasing, engineering, and operations departments must work together to create a successful VA/VE program.

VA/VE in the Supply Chain

There are three primary supply chain areas in which VA/VE can take place. The first is inside the buying organization, the second is at the interface between the suppliers and the buying organization, and the third is inside supplier organizations.

Within the buying organization, often a large group of experts is dedicated to VA/VE activities. This group is usually part of the PSM department. The experts have backgrounds in purchasing and engineering and are adept in communicating with both the buyers and the engineers. For instance, at Harley-Davidson, members of the purchasing staff were assigned to work exclusively on product design and development.[12] At Maytag, the purchasing department organized the early design involvement for its successful Neptune washers. Other leading OEMs are involving their purchasing departments early in the design phase to take advantage of the value that both purchasing and the supply chain can bring to a new product design. The intent is to find cost-saving opportunities that are hidden in the supply chain, and the purchasing department is in the best position to uncover them.

At the interface between buying and supplying organizations, often the buying organization's purchasing and engineering staff works with the supplier's marketing and engineering staff on VA/VE projects. This group may travel to plants belonging to both organizations to observe how a design affects manufacturing and to discuss possibilities for simplifying the design of a product.

Within the supplier organization, engineers and the purchasing staff also engage in VA/VE activities, especially when they are given the task of designing subassemblies and parts by the buying company. According to purchasing managers at Honda, many of the ideas for design improvements that helped reduce the cost of manufacturing the new Accord came from the suppliers.

Process Improvement Programs

VA/VE has typically been focused on the analysis of a product, part, or material. This section looks at a model of process improvement. The model shows how different problem-solving tools and techniques can be aligned with the underlying dynamics of an organization. Based on the general model of process improvement, this section will then consider how purchasing can establish a process improvement program with supplier organizations.

A Model of Process Improvement

All organizations exist because they engage in activities that create value for the customer. These activities are organized around a complex web of processes that create identifiable subproducts, either physical subcomponents (for example, wafer manufacturing in a high-tech company) or segments of a service (for example, application review in an insurance company). The processes also can be a series of activities that must take place to support the creation of the identifiable subproduct (for example, machine maintenance or inventory management). In this vein, Evans and Lindsay defined a process as a "sequence of activities that is intended to achieve some result, typically to create added value for a customer."[13]

The first step in process improvement is the identification of a process that needs improvement. Most purchasing managers have a good idea about which processes require improvement. They often point to the processes that have been falling short of quality, cost, or delivery expectations. These are often bottleneck processes, processes that are overly complex, or processes that result in disgruntled suppliers and show a high turnover. For instance, an inefficient accounts payable process may lead to disgruntled suppliers, and this may negatively affect the supplier relationships that purchasing is trying to build. In such instances, the accounts payable process can be identified as one that needs improvement.

When a purchasing manager identifies a process to analyze, he or she must keep in mind that the process must produce an identifiable result. The manager should give an explicit statement about the output of the process — what identifiable subproduct this process produces (for example, a check for the supplier). The manager should also identify the inputs involved in this process (such as invoices and purchase orders). This first step appears within the process improvement model in Figure 5.1.

FIGURE 5.1
A Process Improvement Model

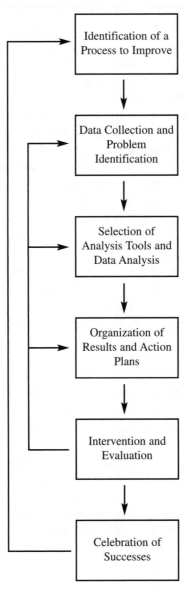

Step two focuses on the nature of the transformation or the added value that occurs within the process. This step involves collecting data on the steps contained in the process. All of the steps should be identified, and the performance indicators for each step should be measured (for example, mean time and the degree of variation measured in standard deviation or simply in range). Flowcharting is an excellent way to gather initial data on the process. A flowchart is a graphic illustration of the sequence of steps performed within a process. Once the basic information is collected and organized into tables and figures, managers can make some basic observations and identify problems. At this point, it is important to state explicitly what the problems are. Managers should ask where the bottleneck exists in the process, because the bottleneck controls the cycle time. Which steps show high mean time or high variation? Where are the complexities, or where do unnecessary steps exist? Are there any excessive queue times (that is, time waiting in queue for processing) or wait times (that is, time expended waiting for dependent processes to complete)?

Once the problems are identified, step three begins. Step three involves applying appropriate data analysis tools. Possible tools that the purchasing manager can use are: Ishikawa problem-solving tools,[14] benchmarking, brainstorming, forecasting tools, and queuing analysis. The problems or the nature of the problems should drive the selection of the tools — the tools should never drive their application to a problem. For example, just because a corporation has a predilection for benchmarking, it should not apply benchmarking every time there is a problem. The tools should be applied systematically, and the problems should always drive the selection of the tools.

All data analysis should be conducted judiciously. The purchasing manager should remember to list the assumptions that underlie the analysis. Does the analysis assume all workers are equally knowledgeable? Are the events that are being considered regarded as dependent or independent events? Are there any underlying probability distributions? Explicit articulation of the assumptions is important because it will affect the interpretation of the results.

Once the analysis is completed and organized, the purchasing manager can set up action plans. At this point, it is important to confirm the integrity of the data collection and analysis. Snap decisions about what the problem is and how to solve it should be avoided before the data collection and analysis is checked.

When action plans are established, they should be implemented, and the results should be evaluated. Depending on the outcome of the evaluation, the purchasing manager could go back to any point in the data collection and analysis procedures and repeat the sequence if he or she feels this is necessary. Once the process is considered a success (no matter how big or how small), it should be celebrated by everyone who had a part in it. This step is often forgotten in the process improvement sequence. Many managers simply rush on to the next project when one project is done. However, in order to foster the spirit of ongoing improvement, an organization should celebrate successes and remember that success begets success.

Supplier Development Process

Process improvement activities that involve purchasing are often extended to the supplier organizations. To harness closer buyer-supplier relationships and to help supplier organizations facilitate their improvement activities, purchasing professionals may visit supplier organizations and engage in hands-on improvement activities. This type of improvement program is known as supplier development.

The model of process improvement discussed previously can be applied to a supplier development program. This is a formal program that involves personnel from both organizations. Hahn, Watts, and Kim defined supplier development as formal activities initiated by buying firms to improve the work processes of existing suppliers.[15] Hartley and Choi reported impressive results from supplier development programs in their study of the automotive industry.[16] They reported that General Motors has conducted supplier development in more than 2,000 supplier firms, with the average productivity improvements at these supplier firms exceeding 50 percent and inventory reductions equaling about 70 percent. Honda of America's supplier development team helped to reduce the cost of improving a welding process by more than $2,000 annually. Also, Deere and Company implemented a similar supplier development program, and when Dave Nelson moved from Honda to Deere, the result was higher factory output and profit margin.[17]

Figure 5.2 illustrates a model of supplier development (SD). The model is built on examples of how the buying companies in the automotive industry (that is, General Motors, Ford, Chrysler, Honda, and Toyota) conducted their supplier development activities.[18] At the core of SD programs are the purchasing professionals who take the lead in bringing together the appropriate people from the buying organization (for example, process engineers, cost analysts, and so on) and working with the supplier organization to assign appropriate people from its side (for example, the supplier's process engineer, line supervisors, and so on).

FIGURE 5.2

A Supplier Development Model

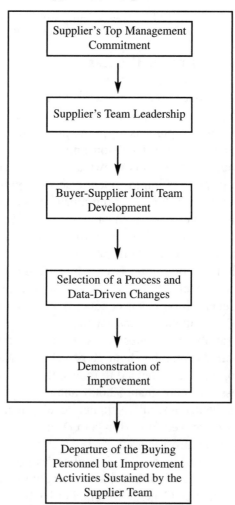

First, the supplier's top management must accept the idea of supplier development. Buying organizations should encourage this idea by expressing interest in long-term relationships and publicizing the importance of SD activities at supplier conferences. Second, to develop a team that can sustain the improvement activities after the buying personnel leave the supplier firm, the purchasing manager from the buying organization typically requests that the supplier assign a person who is knowledgeable and garners respect within the supplier organization to lead the effort. Once this step has been taken, a joint team is organized, and a process is selected. Process selection is analogous to the first step in the process improvement model shown in Figure 5.1. It is important to take care in selecting a process because the joint team must successfully improve this process. Otherwise, once the representatives from the buying organization leave, the SD initiative has virtually no chance of being carried out at the supplier firm.

Then data are collected and analyzed. However, in order to build trust and demonstrate impartiality, all changes must be objective and data-driven (that is, not subjective and value-driven). The joint team must be able to explain objectively why certain changes are being implemented. Here, again, the use of a flowchart plays a key role. Once these changes are made, and success is demonstrated and celebrated, representatives from the buying organization may leave the supplier firm. However, to ensure that improvement activities will be sustained, purchasing managers should continue to maintain communication via phone and regular visits to supplier firms.

Cost Reduction and Avoidance Programs

The VA/VE and process improvement activities discussed earlier in this chapter concern cost reduction and avoidance in one form or another. They try to take out the costs from existing products and processes, as well as from new products and processes.

Typically, in these programs, the target profit for the organization's product lines is based on how much the organization plans to spend for equipment, personnel, and facilities, as well as the market conditions. These target profits must be accomplished through cost-planning activities at the project level. It is at the project level where

target prices are established and cost reduction and avoidance programs must take place. In other words, customer requirements and
target profits are translated into target prices, and the feasibility of
these prices is established through VA/VE and process improvement
activities.

In many organizations, PSM takes a leading role in cost-cutting
programs. For instance, buyers at General Electric, Hewlett-Packard,
Intel, and Motorola led their firms' cost-cutting initiatives.[19] They
used a total cost of ownership (TCO) approach for their sourcing
decisions, which emphasized total costs over the life of purchased
items, rather than price alone. In addition, purchasing departments
used VA/VE to examine decisions on procurement and design at the
piece/part level and to ascertain the value of purchased goods or services compared to their target costs. Another well-known cost-cutting
initiative involving suppliers is Chrysler's (DaimlerChrysler)
Supplier Cost Reduction Effort (SCORE). By sharing the gains from
cost savings with suppliers or giving suppliers additional contracts, or
a combination of both, Chrysler saved about $2 billion when its
annual total budget for procurement was $40 billion.[20]

Cost Improvement Committees

Typically, there are two types of cost improvement committees.
One focuses on purchased parts and raw materials, and the other
focuses on process improvements. Members of the first type of committee hold a series of meetings with the suppliers, and they look for
ways to reduce cost. The second type of committee, which focuses on
process improvements, meets with the internal departments that are
involved in producing the product, and they consider ways to
improve the cost of manufacturing. In either case, the members of
these committees engage in cost improvement activities, such as
reviewing blueprints, revising designs, considering ways to increase
efficiency, testing ideas, and evaluating outcomes.

When members of such committees work on purchased parts and
raw materials, it is often advantageous to involve second-tier suppliers as well. Second-tier suppliers may have lower overheads than
first-tier suppliers, and transferring a task to a second-tier supplier
may lower manufacturing costs. Also, when improving internal

processes, it is critical to involve all departments that are involved in producing a product.

Target Pricing with Suppliers

A buying organization can take a more proactive stance on reducing the cost of purchased parts. The process of target pricing with a supplier is shown in Figure 5.3. The process entails three steps — getting to know the supplier, proposing a target price, and helping the supplier reduce costs and increase its profit margin.

FIGURE 5.3

Process of Target Pricing

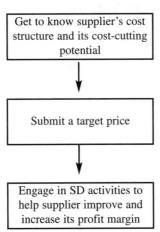

A stamping and welding supplier in Cleveland, Ohio, sought contracts from Honda of America. Before awarding its first job to this supplier, Honda sent representatives from purchasing to reside at the supplier for an entire year.[21] During this year, Honda representatives learned about the supplier's cost structure, as well as the potential for cost reduction (step one).

When Honda finally submitted the target price of the first job to the supplier, this price reflected Honda's knowledge of both the supplier's cost structure and its potential for cost reduction (step two). Once the supplier accepted a price that offered a rather small profit margin, Honda continued to work with this supplier to make improvements that helped the supplier widen the profit margin (step three). Eventually, with a higher efficiency, this supplier also began to enjoy higher profits from its other customers.

Consolidated Supply Strategy

When orders are consolidated to fewer suppliers, opportunities to reduce cost naturally arise. When Deere and Company discovered that it had excessive suppliers (that is, 165 suppliers provided 75 percent of the parts and materials that Deere purchased, while 1,500 suppliers delivered the remaining 15 percent), it reduced its number of suppliers. With a smaller supplier base, Deere was able to undertake a successful cost management program.[22] When Southeastern Freight Lines consolidated the purchase of forms management to one source, it saved 17.5 percent annually for two years.[23] The cost savings came largely from process improvements (for example, more accurate reporting and more efficient inventory management at warehouses).

Foxboro outsourced its maintenance, repair, and operating (MRO) items for its three divisions through a single electrical distributor, Wesco. By contracting with one company, Foxboro was able to reduce its supply base by 500. Wesco, in turn, established alliances with 18 other suppliers to gain leverage on volume and to reduce costs. Consequently, Foxboro reduced its purchasing costs by 15 percent during the first year, 11 percent during the second year, and was expecting to gain another 10 percent reduction during the third year.[24]

Cost savings at Wesco also resulted from systematically applying value engineering to specific products (for example, fasteners and carbide inserts). Foxboro had spent $1.5 million annually to purchase 2,000 different fasteners. Wesco subsequently formed an alliance with Atlantic Fasteners, and engineers from both Foxboro and Atlantic worked together to standardize and reduce their number of parts to 33. This effort saved Foxboro $285,000, and the savings have been projected to eventually reach $430,000, or 30 percent of total costs. Further, using standard fasteners generated additional cost savings by avoiding the creation of new fastener demands for new products.

When value engineering was applied to carbide inserts, Foxboro reduced its supply base from three suppliers to one, and it standardized the carbide inserts and reduced their number from 68 to 37. This effort resulted in a 15 percent cost savings of $500,000 annually. In the end, Wesco provided both fasteners and carbide inserts on a consignment basis. Wesco managed the inventory and replenished it as necessary. Using this approach, Foxboro reduced its costs further because it was not involved in inventory management.

Cost Reduction Targets

Cost reduction targets can be based on a short-term profit plan. An organization can establish an internal goal to reduce either its labor or overhead. Once cost drivers are identified for the activities required to produce specific product lines, a cost reduction target (which can encompass labor, equipment, and other expenses) can be obtained and incorporated into an overall management plan.

Cost reduction targets also can be applied to the purchasing of parts and raw materials. Two approaches have been used to execute these reductions. One approach is to apply a reduction unilaterally to all products purchased from a particular supplier. A few years ago, one leading auto manufacturer imposed a 3-1-1 plan on its suppliers; it demanded that the suppliers render a 3 percent cost reduction in the first year and a 1 percent reduction in each of the two following years.

However, many organizations have abandoned this type of "strong-armed" approach and are working toward a more conciliatory, partnering approach. For example, the buyers at Toshiba Toner Products Division said that unilaterally pressuring suppliers to cut costs jeopardized both opportunities for real cost improvements and its relationship with suppliers.[25] Through its Partners Plus + program, Toshiba focuses on product lines that account for a large portion of its total purchases, such as packaging and raw materials.

In this approach, cost reduction goals typically are targeted toward product types, rather than suppliers. In such cases, the purchasing department would manage the cost of the purchased parts from external suppliers (for example, coating, welding, or raw materials). Activities such as standardization and simplification, SD, VA/VE, and target pricing can be conducive to this approach. For instance, through its total cost management program, Ford Motor Company conducted VA/VE with its suppliers to reduce costs, engaged in SD activities by implementing lean manufacturing practices and process improvements at supplier plants, and exercised a joint effort to reduce the complexity of components and to promote standardization of parts and subsystems.[26] The outcome was significant cost savings, resulting in a 70 percent sharing of components for its new Mercury Cougar line with the Mondeo, Contour, and Mistique platform.

Key Points

1. Simplification is the process of redesigning a product so that it includes fewer varieties of parts or reducing or eliminating marginal product lines.
2. Standardization is a simplification strategy that focuses on increasing the repeated use of components within a product or across different product lines.
3. The ISO is the major international organization dedicated to setting standards for organizations engaged in commerce across international borders. The IEC is another international standard-setting organization; it focuses on electrical, electronic, and related technologies.
4. VA/VE activities focus on designing or redesigning products to reduce their manufacturing cost while maintaining their functionality.
5. When improving a process, it is important to draw boundaries around what the process is, what it does, and what its major inputs and outputs are. As a result, problems can be identified in an objective way, and a concrete measure of improvement is possible.
6. Target costing helps the buyer meet the market requirements for pricing. At the same time, it motivates suppliers to continuously improve their work processes.

Questions for Review

1. What are some of the reasons why the purchasing department should be a part of simplification and standardization?
2. What is the relationship among ISO, IEC, and ANSI?
3. What do ASTM, ASQ, SAE, and ASME have in common in their relationship with ANSI?
4. What key questions should be addressed when conducting a VA/VE analysis?

5. Why should the improvement changes be data-driven instead of intuition- or value-driven?
6. Why is it important to celebrate successes, regardless of how big or small the successes are?
7. Why would a company such as Honda spend one whole year learning about a supplier before awarding a contract to the supplier? How is this answer related to the practice of target costing?

For Additional Information

Banfield, E. "Value Opportunities in the Supply Chain," *Journal of Business Strategy*, May 1999, p. 13.

Brings, J.E. "Metal Standard Designation System," *Standardization News*, September 1994, pp. 20-27.

Jusko, J. "Suppliers in Step," *Industry Week Growing Companies Edition*, April 1999, pp. 32-35.

Kilgore, C., G. Wagner, M. Muller, and C. Hartless, "You Can Get There from Here," *Materials Management in Health Care*, April 1999, pp. 28-30.

Melan, E.H. "Process Management in Service and Administrative Operations," *Quality Progress*, June 1985, pp. 52-59.

Sperati, C.A. "Introducing the United States to the ISO Committee on Terminology (Principles and Coordination)," *ASTM Special Technical Publication*, June 1991, pp. 54-62.

Rowan, C. "Quality and Care: The Key to Innovation," *International Food Ingredients*, May 1999, p. 13.

Wadsworth, H.M. "Making Use of ISO Quality Standards in America," *Annual Quality Congress Transactions*, May 1989, p. 189.

Endnotes

1. Feitzinger, E. and H.L. Lee. "Mass Customization at Hewlett-Packard: The Power of Postponement," *Harvard Business Review*, January-February 1997, pp. 116-121.
2. *Purchasing*. "Supply Strategy Key to Future Growth at Ford," May 7, 1998, pp. 83-84.

3. *International Organization for Standardization.* "What Are Standards," www.iso.ch/infoe/intro.htm, October 1999.
4. *International Electrotechnical Commission.* "Inside the IEC," www.iec.ch, October 1999.
5. *American National Standards Institute.* "An Introduction to ANSI," web.ansi.org/public/about.html, October 1999.
6. *Industrial Agriculture-USA Clearinghouse.* "American Society for Testing and Materials (ASTM)," www.ia-usa.org, October 1999.
7. *American Society for Quality.* "American Society for Quality Origin," www.asq.org, October 1999.
8. *Society of Automotive Engineers.* "About SAE," www.sae.org, October 1999.
9. *American Society for Mechanical Engineers.* "About ASME," www.asme.org, October 1999.
10. Chappell, L. "Deere Sir: Former Honda Sourcing Boss Brings Ideas to New Field," *Automotive News*, (28: 1), 1998.
11. Dobler, D. and D.N. Burt. *Purchasing and Supply Management*, McGraw-Hill, New York, NY, 1996.
12. Fitzgerald, K.R. "Purchasing Unlocks Supply Treasures," *Purchasing*, March 1999, pp. 50-57.
13. Evans, J.R. and W.M. Lindsay, *The Management and Control of Quality*, West Publishing, New York, NY, 1996.
14. Evans, 1996.
15. Hahn, C.K., C.A. Watts, and K.Y. Kim. "The Supplier Management Program: A Conceptual Model," *International Journal of Purchasing and Materials Management*, (26: 2), 1990, pp. 2-7.
16. Hartley, J.L., and T.Y. Choi. "Supplier Development: Customers as a Catalyst of Process Change," *Business Horizons*, July-August 1996, pp. 37-44.
17. Hartley and Choi, 1996.
18. Hartley and Choi, 1996.
19. Minahan, T. "Buyers Take a Lead Role in Setting Corporate Strategies," *Purchasing*, (120: 7), 1996, p. 31.
20. Stone, S. "DaimlerChrysler Uses One Global Strategy," *Purchasing*, (14), 1999, p. 109.

21. Choi, T.Y. "Learning Quality Techniques from Target Stamping," in J. Heizer and J. Nathan (Eds.), *Cases in Total Quality Management*, 1998.
22. Choi, 1998.
23. Avery, S. "Outsourcing Helps Cut Forms Purchasing Costs," *Purchasing*, May 1999, pp. 93-98.
24. Avery, S. "Integrate Supply: Value Engineering Reduces Costs," *Purchasing*, (125: 6), 1998, pp. 102-105.
25. Avery, S. "Toshiba Program Rewards Suppliers for New Ideas," *Purchasing*, May 1999, pp. 24-26.
26. Avery, 1999, p. 24-26.

CHAPTER 6

THE ROLE OF PURCHASING AND SUPPLY IN NEW PRODUCT DEVELOPMENT

What is the best way for purchasing and supply management to have a positive impact on new product/service design and development?

Chapter Objectives

- To understand the contribution that purchasing can make to new product and service design
- To be able to develop strategies to encourage earlier purchasing involvement in the design and development process
- To understand the importance of early supplier involvement in new product/service design and development
- To be able to distinguish among the elements of early supplier involvement
- To understand the risks of not getting purchasing and suppliers involved early
- To be able to work with suppliers to encourage mutual disclosure of confidential information within a legal framework that protects all parties

Introduction

Early purchasing and supplier involvement has achieved buzzword status in business today. While some organizations have made progress in terms of getting purchasing and suppliers involved early in the design process, this is certainly not true in general. This chapter explores a number of issues related to early purchasing and supplier involvement, including the following: How early is early enough for purchasing and suppliers to be involved? Why is early purchasing and supplier involvement important? How can purchasing make the greatest possible contribution to the organization's design and development process?

The Opportunity of Early Purchasing Involvement

One of the great challenges in business and government today is for organizations to use technology to compete in world markets. This involves designing better, higher-quality products and getting them to market quickly, before the competition. Purchasing can play a pivotal role in coordinating the transition of new products from the development stage to the production stage.

Concurrent Engineering

Concurrent engineering is a manufacturing strategy that can provide the manufacturer with a competitive advantage in the world marketplace. *Concurrent engineering*, also referred to as *simultaneous engineering*, is a process in which a team (or teams) simultaneously designs a product and its supporting production process. By considering product attributes, such as manufacturability, procurability, reliability, maintainability, schedulability, marketability, and disassembly, in the early stages of product design, many problems and delays can be prevented as the product enters the production stage. In a recent survey, only about half of the respondents indicated that they use concurrent engineering.[1]

Early Purchasing Involvement and Concurrent Engineering

The focal point of concurrent design is product or service design. Any decision concerning product design may have far-reaching effects on the product's long-term cost and viability. Figure 6.1 is a widely used figure that shows the impact of design on the cost of a product or service over its life cycle. This figure shows that while design costs may account for only 5 to 15 percent of the total expenditure on a product or service, design directly influences about 70 percent of all other costs. In other words, once a product or service has been designed, most of the costs of that product or service have been determined.

FIGURE 6.1

Design for Competitiveness: A Powerful Manufacturing Strategy
Percent of Influence — Manufacturing or
Service Delivery Costs

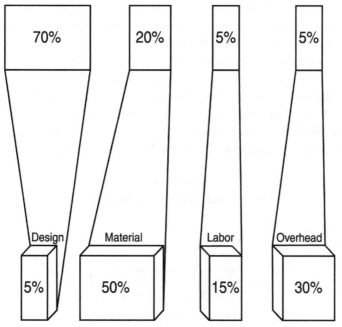

Percent of Product or Service Cost from a Xerox Example

Thus, if the initial design is bad, the organization will end up paying for it again, and again, and again. There is a joke of sorts about design changes in the automotive and aerospace industries: Historically, the specifications for parts change so many times from the original drawing to the final part (each change is known as an engineering change order), that the price of the part or component could increase 10 to 50 percent before an end product is produced. The supplier can "low-ball" the initial price, knowing it will have numerous opportunities to inflate the price as changes develop. The role of the supplier and how this price acceleration can be prevented are presented in more depth in the sections on target costing and early supplier involvement.

Areas of Purchasing and Design Synergy

There are a number of areas where it is crucial for purchasing to work closely with the design function, beyond those mentioned previously. Each of these major areas is presented in the following sections.

Research and Development

As soon as the design function begins to conceptualize a new product or service idea, purchasing should be consulted. The purchaser could provide insights and begin to identify potential sources. Both the design and purchasing functions bring valuable information to the development process. Working together improves the speed of release, cost-effectiveness, and the total quality of a new product (see Figure 6.2).

FIGURE 6.2
Design and Purchasing Interface

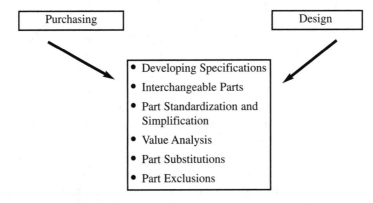

| Purchasing | | Design |

- Developing Specifications
- Interchangeable Parts
- Part Standardization and Simplification
- Value Analysis
- Part Substitutions
- Part Exclusions

Purchasing Orientation	Design Orientation
1. Minimum acceptable margins of quality, safety, and performance	1. Wider margins of quality, safety, and performance
2. Use of adequate materials	2. Use of ideal materials
3. Lowest ultimate costs	3. Limited concern for cost
4. High regard for availability	4. Limited regard for availability
5. Practical and economical parameters, specifications, features, and tolerances	5. Close or near-perfect parameters, specifications, features, and tolerances
6. General view of product quality	6. Conceptual abstraction of product quality
7. Cost estimation of materials	7. Selection of materials
8. Concern for JIT delivery and supplier relationship	8. Concern for overall product design

At Harley-Davidson, purchasing, engineering, and manufacturing have equal say on all aspects of product design. This more fully uses purchasing's skills and increases supplier involvement. A number of purchasing professionals have been assigned to work exclusively on a product's design and development.[2] Purchasing's involvement in design is part of Harley-Davidson's overall strategy to get new products to market faster, with higher quality and a lower cost. But purchasing's involvement in design is not limited to the manufacturing sector. For example, at Commercial Financial Services (CFS), a company that deals with charged-off credit card loans, purchasing gets involved very early in identifying needs with its technical group. Dave Jewitt, CFS' purchasing director, says, "Early on, we ask our technical people about their requirements and about the need they hope each piece of equipment will meet. Then, we can carry the load in the acquisition process."[3]

Caterpillar created an early supplier involvement group to act as a liaison between Caterpillar's product design group and the main purchasing organization. Purchasing plays a key role in bringing suppliers and designers together and educating engineers regarding suppliers' capabilities.[4]

Design for Manufacturability, Assembly, and Delivery

Crucial to the success of concurrent engineering is the principle of design for manufacturability, assembly, and/or delivery. In this principle of design, engineering works with purchasing, manufacturing, operations, and marketing on the front end. The supplier may also be involved.

Design for delivery considers the handling of the end product — packaging and delivery to ensure the product is not damaged, efficient uses of storage/transit space, and ease of unpacking. Unpacking is often an important concern for consumer products that may be unpacked for display right on the display floor.

The goal of design for manufacturability is to simplify the manufacturing process by improving the product design. Table 6.1 provides a summary of the key steps in design for manufacturability. Simply put, design a product so it is easy to manufacture and/or assemble. This avoids errors that waste time and resources later in the product's life cycle. Design for manufacturability includes such elements as reducing the number of parts. Design for assembly goes hand-in-hand with design for manufacturability, and it also considers the ease of handling and assembling parts and components.

TABLE 6.1
Key Steps in Design for Manufacturability

1. Analyze the architectural design of processes and production in order to identify fundamental problems. Then, scrutinize the details of the design of products and the processes in place to produce them.

2. Break down the products and process systems into their component parts or subsystems, and identify the interactions among them.

3. Align the requirements for the design of the product with those for the process design and organizational structure.

4. Explore alternatives for the primary product design process and manufacturing processes.

5. Estimate early for the costs of adopting various process options.

6. Estimate early for the time requirements — in person-hours, but especially in the critical path time effects — of executing different design options.

7. Identify and alleviate any bottlenecks in the CE process.

8. Manage the design process with multifunctional teams working concurrently.

9. Align incentives for design such that tradeoffs associated with selecting alternative design options will be made from a global, product life cycle perspective.

Source: Charles Fine, Clockspeed, Perseus Book, Reading, MA, 1998, pp. 132-133.

Design for the Environment

Design for the environment initiatives include design for disassembly and reuse, as well as design for waste minimization. These initiatives are self-explanatory: designing processes and products so that there is minimal waste in production, and so that they can be disassembled in order to be recycled, reused, or disposed of in the most environmentally conscious way possible. This approach is not only good for the environment, it also is the ultimate in forward-thinking supply chain management, because it embraces the "dust to dust" or "cradle to grave" concepts espoused by supply chain management. Design for the environment is becoming increasingly common as organizations are subject to more environmental legislation and greater environmental consciousness.

Walton, Handfield, and Melnyk suggest two proactive guidelines for purchasing and supplier involvement in design for the environment:[5]

1. Product design and purchasing personnel should work together to influence environmental improvements in their own and their supplier's products. This can be achieved by substituting or changing materials specifications for purchased products and avoiding the use of hazardous or EPA-regulated materials where possible, to reflect the environmental agenda of the company.

2. Product design processes must consider the life cycle of all materials used in the product, including cradle to grave considerations. This can be accomplished by promoting dialogue between designers and materials experts and the use of tools, such as life cycle analysis, quality functional deployment, and design for environment by cross-functional teams.

In a recent survey, nearly half of the manufacturers polled on environmental manufacturing practices identified suppliers as key players in pollution prevention.[6] For example, Procter has been working with its supply base to reduce waste in consumer packaging since 1988. Its approach uses both material reduction and recycling efforts. The organization has introduced these packaging issues into consumer focus groups and integrated the results into its new product development process.[7] Clearly, it is critical to involve purchasing and suppliers in the process of design for the environment.

Substitution

Purchasing can recommend parts that meet functional requirements at the lowest total cost. The purchaser is often most familiar with the parts and components in use by the organization, because she or he buys the items on a regular basis. Purchasing may also be aware of good suppliers in relevant industries. Potential suppliers that are contacted early can often recommend newer or alternative components that may meet the needs more effectively than those in the proposed design. It is critical to incorporate innovative ideas before a design is finalized, because proposed substitutes may affect other aspects of the design.

Product Innovation

Suppliers are the experts in their area. If the suppliers do not know more about their industry than the organization does, perhaps the organization is working with the wrong suppliers. Suppliers may be able to recommend new solutions and approaches that enable designers to make inventive or resourceful changes to a product. For example, Phelps Dodge Mining Corporation and Michelin Tire have a symbiotic supply relationship. Michelin provides Phelps Dodge with its latest tire technology for use at Phelps Dodge mines. In turn, Phelps Dodge gives Michelin access to the tires while they are in use, so that Michelin can test them under various conditions and provide continuous improvement. Michelin, the tire expert, keeps Phelps Dodge up-to-date on the latest products and substitutes. Both parties benefit, and the cooperation enhances product development.

In the automotive sector, companies have grown increasingly reliant upon suppliers for product innovations with excellent results. Nelson, Mayo, and Moody report that at Honda, "purchasing encourages suppliers to rethink design details; suppliers are expected to 'lead the way' in new process and product technologies."[8]

Contracting for Design Services

During the design phase of new product or service development, scarce project resources may delay the new product's introduction.

These resources can include specialists to work on packaging design and market research, circuit design, software development and programming, prototype machining and assembly, graphic design, technical writing, modeling, tests, and equipment rental. Purchasing can reduce this risk by monitoring the project results and developing contractual relationships with outside service providers. A major electronics manufacturer has a formalized risk process managed by purchasing to help identify and solve any such problems before they could lead to delays in a new product's development and introduction.[9]

Qualified Products and Qualified Suppliers List

Purchasing can help prevent delays in the rollout of new products or services by calling attention to parts with long or unstable lead-times, and problem suppliers. The speed of the entire process is dependent on the weakest link in the process. It is advisable to avoid parts or processes that may impede the smooth flow of the operation. Specifically identifying and monitoring high-risk parts and components is part of the electronics manufacturer's risk management process mentioned previously. The process includes identifying the potential "show stoppers" that could delay the new product's development or rollout. Purchasing is also responsible for identifying suppliers with whom the organization has had a history of poor performance, or suppliers that are financially unstable. These suppliers should be avoided if possible.[10]

Early Supplier Involvement (ESI)

ESI is a practice that involves one or more selected suppliers with a purchaser's product design team early in the specification development process. The objective is to use the supplier's expertise and experience in developing a product or service specification that is designed for effective and efficient manufacturability, assembly, and delivery. As discussed earlier in this chapter, many of the benefits of early purchasing involvement in design are derived from purchasing's intimate knowledge of the supply base, as well as purchasing's knowledge of when it is advisable to involve suppliers early and the extent of that involvement. One of the key characteristics of "best-in-class" purchasing is that purchasing "leverages the suppliers' value-added capabilities for logistics, design, and materials handling."[11]

For example, at Texas Instruments, major suppliers are selected and integrated at the design stage, before the system has been defined. A major benefit is that the problems found during production definition and design are much easier and less expensive to fix.[12]

Sourcing and Cost/Profitability Issues

As presented in the section on concurrent engineering, purchasing can make the greatest contribution if it is involved early in a product design project to make sure all potential costs are identified accurately. The way that Intel views purchasing's potential contribution to the design process is illustrated in Figure 6.3. While it may seem extreme in some industries that the relative value of purchasing's contribution drops so sharply once the contract has been signed, it makes sense for a number of reasons.

FIGURE 6.3
Value of Pre-Positioning the Supply Chain

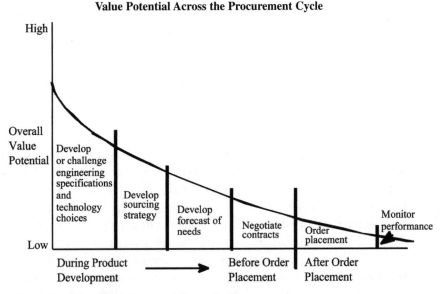

Value Potential Across the Procurement Cycle

*Source: Capital Consulting & Management, Inc., used by Intel
Used by permission of the Center for Advanced Purchasing Studies

As pointed out previously, most of the cost of a system, process, product, or service is determined during the design phase. Thus, if purchasing is not involved at the design stage, a significant portion of its opportunity to contribute is missed. Purchasing can still make an excellent contribution by developing the sourcing strategy (that is, which suppliers, how many, and what type of relationship) and forecasting future needs. Purchasing can also contribute, although to a lesser degree, through effective negotiations. In many cases, the requirements and flexibility are limited after the design phase, especially if this stage is purchasing's first involvement. Setting up the means for order placement and management (supplier-managed inventory, e-commerce, blanket orders, and so on) also makes a contribution. Once purchasing is monitoring performance, the value it adds is the lowest, because it is just monitoring progress and correcting problems that should have been prevented through early involvement.

The reason that the "monitoring performance" contribution is so low for a company like Intel is that its product life cycles are short. If it doesn't "get it right the first time," there may be no time or value to fixing it, because the product may be obsolete by the time the problem is fixed. This is not as true for companies with longer life-cycle products, such as the automotive industry. For example, DaimlerChrysler's SCORE program, which focuses on supplier cost reduction efforts primarily for existing products, saved approximately $2 billion in 1998.[13] Thus, the potential for savings may still exist once a product or service is in production. However, anything that can be saved "after the fact" could have saved even more, if it had been integrated into the initial design process.

Target Costing

Companies often integrate the concept of target costing along with concurrent engineering. This helps to provide a cost goal and to manage the production cost of the product or service. Target costing is an emerging process through which the organization calculates the allowable cost for buying/manufacturing the product or service it offers for sale. First, the organization determines the acceptable selling price in the marketplace, and then it subtracts the organization's required internal margin on the product. The equation follows:

Target Cost = Price – Desired Profit Margin

Within the target cost, all of the organization's costs of business — including sales, marketing, distribution, production, labor, and materials costs — must be accounted for. A cross-functional team generally works to apportion all of the costs to the various units. Purchasing gets one piece of that cost, which must be further broken down into the various purchased elements. An example of how this breakdown occurs for one automotive manufacturer is shown in Figure 6.4.

FIGURE 6.4

Target Cost Breakdown at Automotive Manufacturer

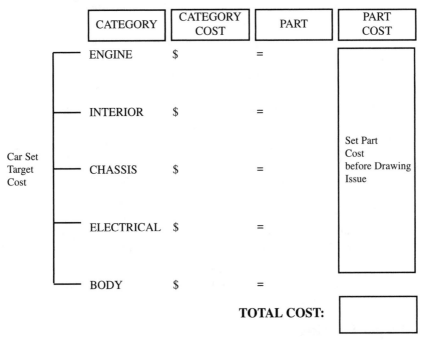

CATEGORY	CATEGORY COST	PART	PART COST
ENGINE	$	=	
INTERIOR	$	=	
CHASSIS	$	=	Set Part Cost before Drawing Issue
ELECTRICAL	$	=	
BODY	$	=	
		TOTAL COST:	

Car Set Target Cost

Source: *The Role of Supply Management in Target Costing.* Center for Advanced Purchasing Studies and the National Association of Purchasing Management, Tempe, AZ, 1999, p. 91.

Clearly, in order for target costing to be effective, purchasing must be part of the design team. Purchasing should work with the designers to make modifications as necessary to fulfill the functional requirements of the part or service, while still meeting the target cost. Purchasing could not effectively support target costing if the design was simply "thrown over the wall," and purchasing had to work on its own to achieve the target. Target costing is generally an iterative process that requires great supplier involvement. The steps in the target costing process are illustrated in Figure 6.5. In cases where the target cost cannot be met by the time required for the new product or service rollout, the organization must decide what approach to take. Should it cancel the new product or service offering? This is the best decision if the introduction would result in a loss. Should it delay rollout? This can be costly, due to the time-to-market issues. Should it introduce the new product or service anyway? This approach is common. However, if target costs are not met, the product team, including purchasing, will continue to work toward cost reduction and meeting the targets. In addition, the targets will change and be reduced over time as the product or service matures. Target costing is an ongoing process.

Target costing is valuable in supporting the organization's overall efforts to remain cost competitive while meeting the customer's demands. Yet target costing is not a stand-alone effort. It is a process most effectively undertaken by cross-functional teams, in conjunction with other value-adding processes, such as early supplier involvement, value analysis, and value engineering.

Organizations choose to use target costing for a variety of reasons. The reasons may be broadly classified as the need to increase competitiveness. An organization may desire to increase communication and early supplier involvement in its new product or service development process, thereby leveraging some of the supplier's expertise. In addition, there are cost management reasons for implementing target costing, such as cost reduction and improved understanding of the supplier's cost structures, as well as improving internal cost management, improving cost monitoring, and increasing cost accountability. Reasons for choosing target costing, based on a recent study, are listed in Table 6.2. Virtually all of the organizations studied have multiple objectives for target costing; target costing is not a tool or process that is used in isolation. Target costing is an important building block in the new product development process.

FIGURE 6.5
Target Costing Process

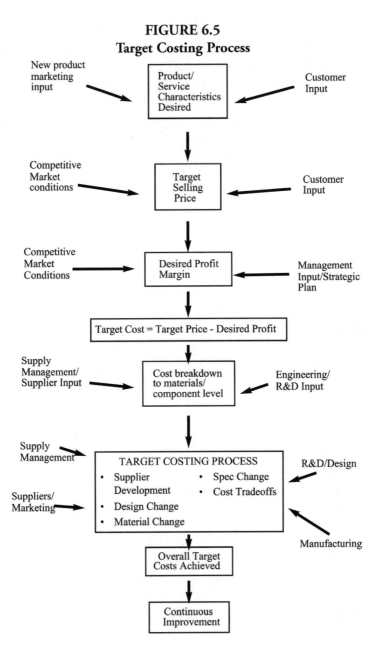

Source: *The Role of Supply Management in Target Costing.* Center for Advanced Purchasing
Studies and the National Association of Purchasing Management, Tempe, AZ, 1999, p. 16.

TABLE 6.2
Reasons for Target Costing

Cost Reduction

- As a way to work more closely with suppliers on cost reduction
- In response to greater cost/price pressure from the market, customers, or competitors
- To provide suppliers a target (they did not want to voluntarily reduce price)

Cost Disclosure and Understanding

- As a way to encourage suppliers to share cost data
- To allow a better understanding of cost drivers
- To better understand supplier cost structure

Continuous Improvement/Competitiveness

- To facilitate the culture change from an engineering-driven company to a product-driven or customer-driven company
- To be more competitive in a changing regulatory environment
- To help identify specific areas for improvement
- As an integral part of the organization's continuous improvement philosophy

Improved Communications and Early Involvement

- As a means of getting purchasing and suppliers involved earlier in new product development
- Needed a target price for suppliers to shoot for as the organization shifts from an industrial to a consumer market
- To facilitate supplier negotiations
- To have a common goal for the new product development team

Improved Design and Accountability

- To design the right products at the right price before they go to market, supporting value-engineering efforts
- To create accountability for costs from design and procurement
- To provide a benchmark against which to measure the organization's and suppliers' performance

Source: The Role of Supply Management in Target Costing. Center for Advanced Purchasing Studies and the National Association of Purchasing Management, Tempe, AZ, 1999, p. 26.

The concept of target costing is not just for manufactured items, although that has been its primary application. Target costing is also used in purchasing services, including advertising services, maintenance, and contracted support services. The applications of target costing are limited only by the imagination.

Accountability for results is key to the long-term success of target costing. A primary way to create accountability is by holding regular meetings to discuss progress throughout the new product or service development cycle. Involvement in target costing represents a positive way for purchasing to contribute to organizational success and to be involved early in product/service development. Target costing is just one tool of many to improve organizational competitiveness and to increase purchasing and supplier involvement throughout all stages of product/service development.

Speed to Market

Speed to market was the battle cry of the 1990s, and it continues to be an important issue. Global competition, accelerated technological advances, and market demands for new merchandise and services are among the reasons to reduce product or service to market lead-times. The two critical aspects of speed to market are the time it takes to develop and introduce a new product or service and the time that an item spends in the "pipeline," before it is actually sold or otherwise consumed or disposed of. Organizations want to improve management of both aspects of speed to market.

Purchasing must take an active role in new product development through its cooperation in cross-functional teams. This participation can reduce time-to-market and increase product acceptability in the marketplace. Purchasing's crucial contributions are in the early identification and qualification of suppliers that are able to provide a continuous supply of materials, components, and services, and in bringing the right suppliers into the design process early.

DaimlerChrysler made a last-minute change to the roof control unit in its V Class van (produced in Europe). It was told that it would be impossible for the project to meet its deadlines, because the roof module was complex and required integration with many other interfaces. The chosen supplier took control of the situation, produced the item on time, and met all of DaimlerChrysler's requirements. Had

DaimlerChrysler tried to design the item or have too much control of the process, it would not have been successful.[14] The more time that an organization takes to introduce a new product or service, the longer productive assets are tied up in the development process and the greater the expense. At AlliedSignal's engine business, new engine development costs about $1 million per week. Each week that development can be reduced frees up assets, and the assets can be put to other uses.[15]

As part of the early supplier involvement process, purchasing must identify the right types of relationships to have with suppliers. Early supplier involvement and joint product/process development often involve a supplier alliance or partnership, which is presented in greater depth in the second volume in this series. Alliances tend to be long-term, cooperative relationships yielding mutual benefits to both the buying and supplying organizations.

Taking cycle time or leadtime out of the pipeline, from identifying the need for the product/service through delivery to the customer, can occur at any point during a product or service life cycle. However, such initiatives are most effectively built in during product or service development. Some of the ways to reduce cycle time include the following:

- Improve forecasting accuracy (see Chapter 7)
- Simplify and standardize parts and components (see Chapter 4)
- Select suppliers in close physical proximity to the production or service delivery location
- Improve information flow from customers and to suppliers
- Identify risk areas in new product/service development and create contingency plans
- Reduce waste and work-in-process inventory
- Design flexible systems

Some of these issues should be dealt with and planned for when the product or service is being developed. An organization should be thinking about all aspects of its supply chain design while it is developing new products or services; it should be "designing for supply chain management."

Supplier Development

A qualified base of suppliers may not be available to support the organization's needs for new or existing purchases. If this is the case, supplier development may be necessary. When Honda of America Manufacturing first came to the United States, it discovered that finding suppliers to meet its quality, delivery, service, and price needs was difficult. Honda purchasing and engineering personnel worked closely with many suppliers to develop the suppliers' skills at the same time that Honda was developing its products in the United States. This is a long-term investment. Through early involvement in the design process, purchasing can identify gaps between the abilities of available suppliers and the organization's needs. Purchasing can then work to develop suppliers to minimize the potential delays in a new product or service rollout.

Early Involvement in Capital Acquisitions

Purchasing can make the most significant contribution to the capital budget and approval process if it is involved in the capital needs assessment. Capital evaluation often involves a team that includes purchasing, engineering, manufacturing, and the user department that is developing the need. The purchaser who is aware of a need for a capital asset can develop a list of suppliers that can satisfy the need. This not only speeds up the development of a capital project proposal, but it also shortens the later acquisition process.

The approval, acquisition, installation, and ramp-up for productive capital can be a lengthy process. Forecasting a need for equipment or facilities allows potential suppliers to allocate manufacturing or human resource time in advance of the need. This will also speed up the acquisition process for items with long leadtimes. Capital asset availability can provide a competitive advantage in the introduction of new products. Intel spent billions of dollars on buildings and equipment between 1996 and 1998 in anticipation of the growth in semiconductor demand from 1997 to 1999. Intel's accurate assessment of the market and preparation for the demand allowed it to experience tremendous sales growth that would not have been otherwise possible. Intel was ready to take advantage of the window of opportunity.

Other Purchasing Synergism in New Product or Service Development

Additional areas of collaboration for purchasing on the design team include the development of specifications, part standardization and simplification, value analysis, part substitutions, and part exclusions. New product development efforts must take advantage of the "strategic positioning" aspect of the purchasing operation. Suppliers must also be considered critical members of this team. Purchasing is pivotal to the exchange of useful information between the supplier and the end user. The issue of earlier supplier involvement is addressed more fully in the next section.

The Importance of Early Supplier Involvement

As introduced earlier in this chapter, suppliers play an increasingly important role in product development for many organizations. One example is the role that early supplier involvement had at Chrysler; suppliers are given significant credit for the turnaround of this once-ailing company. In the late 1980s, after being bailed out of bankruptcy by the U.S. government, Chrysler knew that it needed to significantly reduce its new product development time in order to compete effectively with Japanese and other U.S. auto makers. Its new model development time was then four to six years. Due to market and financial pressures, it had to complete the design to market process in three years.

Chrysler formed cross-functional platform teams and gave each team ownership for one platform: Jeep, minivan, large car, and small car. It also involved its suppliers, and integrated everyone in a single facility that was linked by common software. Chrysler produced its successful LH line, including the Intrepid, New Yorker, and Concorde, in record time. It met its time to market goal, and did it with 30 percent less money invested than any previous platform.[16] Chrysler's suppliers were key to its success. Chrysler's early supplier involvement and the involvement of suppliers on teams continue to grow and flourish.

The Role of the Team in Early Supplier Involvement

As in the Chrysler example discussed previously, more companies are seeing the value of involving their suppliers as members of working teams. The successful organization is one that works as a team. A team functions most effectively when all of its members understand the overall strategy and objectives of the team and the organization it supports.

As a boundary-spanning function, one of purchasing's roles is to act as a key interface with the world outside the organization — disseminating and gathering knowledge and information. Purchasers are responsible for managing the "front end" of a business, and they are the primary contacts with the organization's suppliers. It is the responsibility of purchasing to keep suppliers up-to-date regarding future organizational needs, which enables the suppliers to provide their technological expertise and to support an organization's goals. For example, at Pratt and Whitney, an engine manufacturer, suppliers have been given the responsibility to do more. In the past, Pratt and Whitney did all of its own engine design and manufacturing. Today, two-thirds of the engine is purchased, and three-quarters of the cost comes from outside of purchases.[17] This has shifted the supplier's role from giving the customer what it asks for to telling the customer what it needs to do to stay ahead.

The following sections present areas in which early supplier involvement can enhance the procurement process.

Manufacturing Process

As mentioned previously, suppliers should be experts in their lines of business. An organization's knowledge of its supplier's and customer's manufacturing procedures is important in the development of the most effective process to produce a product or develop a service. Purchasers and suppliers working together can eliminate many cost redundancies. For instance, an organization can buy a product that is semifinished and introduce it to its process at an earlier stage, or a supplier can assume some of the customer's operations, if doing so would lead to lower costs and improved quality. A buying organization has a greater opportunity to come up with cost efficiencies when it understands the supplier's processes and the supplier understands the buying organization's processes. Significant time and money can be saved if the supplier is "on the team" early in the development of the manufacturing process.

In its refrigerated biscuit operations, the Pillsbury Company uses paperboard cans with metal ends. When empty, the cans are relatively light, but they are bulky, expensive to handle, and easily damaged. Understanding this, Pillsbury worked with its can supplier, Boise Cascade, and the can supplier built a factory attached to Pillsbury's refrigerated biscuit factory in New Albany, Indiana. This arrangement was beneficial for both parties. Boise Cascade produced the cans, applied the proper labels, and transported the cans through the adjoining factory wall. This limited Boise's need to store and ship cans, as well as reducing the opportunity for damage. Pillsbury saved also in handling, transportation, and storage. Working together and understanding the other's operations made this synergy possible.

The concept of postponement has become popular in recent years. *Postponement* involves delaying the differentiation of a product to meet the needs of a specific customer for as long as possible. Once a product has been customized to meet a specific order, it is more valuable, and thus ties up more capital. It is also more difficult to sell to someone else. For example, Green Giant does not put specific labels on its canned vegetables until it receives an order, which allows the vegetables to be sold under the Green Giant name or another brand name, if necessary. By understanding other organizations' processes, buyers and suppliers can determine such opportunities.

Capital Acquisitions

Suppliers can also suggest the types of equipment that an organization might use to be more compatible with their processes. This can be helpful when a buying organization is making a capital investment for a new product or process. Suppliers may be familiar with the pros and cons of various equipment manufacturers, either from experience or through other customers' experience. For complex capital purchases, such as building a new plant, suppliers may need to be involved early in the planning process so that they know how their equipment will fit with other equipment, the type of space it will be in, and when it needs to be delivered. Suppliers may be able to identify potential problems in the plan or layout that can be prevented, which may save time and money as the plant becomes operational.

Product or Service Development/Implementation

Suppliers can assist in early product development by providing prototypes, models, or preproduction samples for testing or use in the customer's product development cycle. Good communication and feedback between the customer and the supplier are important. In some cases, such as in the development of a complex new product (for example, an automobile), it is wise to have suppliers of related parts work together to verify the functionality and fit of their parts. Chrysler's platform teams use this concept.

Cost Management

Even before the buying organization presents target cost proposals to suppliers, suppliers can provide useful insights into the costs of manufacturing a product. Suppliers can also provide realistic assessments of what the product development will entail before the product is introduced into the market or purchased by the buying organization. The attainment of cost projections on a new product from a supplier can save an organization from making expensive errors. Further, as mentioned in the section on target costing, suppliers can suggest innovative ideas to allow the buying organization to meet, or perhaps exceed, its cost targets. AlliedSignal Aerospace worked with Howbeit Dover, a supplier, to develop an alternative duct configuration. The jointly developed approach saves AlliedSignal $440,000 per year.[18]

Quality

Involving suppliers early in the development of specifications for products and processes will help reduce the costs of quality of the product or service. Suppliers can help the organization develop quality requirements that will serve the customer in the most effective manner. If suppliers are aware of a customer's needs, they can prepare their organizations to satisfy those needs through human resource development and training, process development and capability studies, equipment acquisition, and other means. Quality is the result of preplanning and preparation. Suppliers that know the future quality requirements can eliminate problems that lead to rejections or rework at later stages. Further, if the supplier understands the buying organization's quality requirements, it can ensure that quality is not being over-specified, which can result in parts and processes that add cost rather than adding value. As mentioned previously in regard to the importance of the design phase, the key is to get it right the first time.

Availability

Suppliers need to have the capacity to serve a customer's needs in a timely manner. If a supplier is aware of forecasted needs, it can let the potential customer know what support it can provide. Purchasers have the responsibility to work with their internal customers to provide forecasted data to the supplier base. This will help eliminate future supplier delivery problems.

In addition to providing accurate forecasting of needs for new products, it is critical to let the supplier know current needs as soon as the information is available. Many organizations have secure Internet sites that provide suppliers with volume forecasts specific to them, as well as future plans for new products. Both Deere and Company and Intel have such sites. These organizations also hold annual, or more frequent, meetings with key suppliers to inform them about "the state of the industry/company." The meetings keep suppliers abreast of plans so that they can be responsive rather than reactive. This is a change from the 1980s when many organizations operated under fear-based environments, with a belief that any information provided to the supplier would be used against the purchaser and the purchaser's organization.

Technology

Supplier expertise can be helpful to designers and will increase their chances of producing a quality, cost-effective product early in the design-marketing cycle. Suppliers can assist in material selection and a host of other areas where designers may not have broad knowledge. Purchasing can assist in this transfer of information by bringing together an organization's technical people with qualified supplier personnel. However, such exchanges can take place only if the supplier feels there is a chance to develop future business. Thus, the purchaser and the designers should agree on a group of suppliers that they are willing to work with early in the process. As pointed out by Ronald Schuster, a purchasing director at General Motors, early supplier involvement with purchasing is important "to make sure that we know all the new products, technologies, and processes while the vehicle is being designed. That's where we get the biggest bang for our buck."[19]

All of the auto makers are involved in early supplier involvement initiatives to improve materials technology. Mark Casey, a purchasing manager at Ford, says, "We are pretty excited about the way we are already working together internally and with our materials suppliers on next-generation vehicles. We've got people from the various metals and plastics companies sitting side-by-side with our design and manufacturing engineers and purchasing personnel so they can help us optimize the efficiency, weight, and performance of vehicles in the future."

Design

Suppliers can provide key elements to a product's design, based on their technical expertise as well as their experience in serving a particular market. Purchasers that maintain long-term relationships with suppliers can often have their designers seek advice from suppliers, with the understanding that the suppliers' technology must be protected. Also, it is important for the supplier to have a reasonable opportunity for gaining business from this activity.

The following list defines several ways that an organization can involve suppliers in design:

- **No Involvement** – The supplier has no input into design. The supplier is expected to provide the buying organization with the item as specified.
- **White Box** – Information from informal discussions and consultations with the supplier may be integrated into the design, but no formal collaboration occurs.
- **Gray Box** – The supplier is integrated into the design teams, such as with concurrent engineering. Design is a joint and collaborative effort that involves the buying organization and its suppliers.
- **Black Box** – The buying organization gives the supplier some general performance specifications and interface requirements. Then, the supplier designs and delivers the required item.[20]

There is no right or wrong approach to involving suppliers in the design process. It depends on the situation. When the organization has world-class expertise or no expertise, it should not involve the supplier in design or it should turn the design over to the supplier, respectively. In many cases, the opportunity for synergy exists. The white box method can be a place to begin, evolving into a fully integrated team approach, as suggested by the gray box.

Product Co-Development

Using suppliers in the co-development of a product or service provides for a sharing of development costs. This normally implies that there is a formal agreement regarding the future business that may result from the development. This agreement can take many forms. The organization can pay the supplier for the development costs, pay a royalty on each item sold, or guarantee a certain amount of future business. Co-development spreads the risk among the organizations involved. It also implies that the rewards will be shared. This may be the only way that a supplier will share technology.

Cycle Time

From a traditional purchasing perspective, cycle time is the period of time between the order and when the item is received and made available for use. A broader perspective of cycle time includes the time from the earliest recognition of the need until the item is received by or the service is provided to the ultimate customer. This broader perspective of cycle time is better because this cycle time is relevant to the customer, and this is how the customer will judge the organization's service. Cycle time can be reduced by the early development of relationships with suppliers. Suppliers can help the organization eliminate redundancies in inbound material handling, quality inspections, manufacturing, and distribution processes. Once the products and processes are in place, the cycle time required to satisfy the ultimate customer with the desired product can be continuously improved. AlliedSignal uses on-site development teams to work with suppliers on improving quality and cycle times. It is not unusual for the supplier to reduce the cost of quality and cut leadtimes by 75 percent.[21] Clearly, the buying and supply organizations can work together to reduce waste and inefficiency in the process, which provides better service to the ultimate customer.

Continuous Improvement

Early supplier involvement paves the way for relationship building with suppliers and supplier involvement in continuous improvement efforts. All of the auto makers have formalized cost savings programs in which they work with suppliers and solicit supplier suggestions for taking costs out of systems. AlliedSignal Supplier Productivity Improvement Results (ASPIRE) is one such supplier suggestion program. It saved AlliedSignal's aerospace group more than $28 million in the five years since its inception. Supplier proposals include ideas on how to reduce the cost of parts, freight, and assembly.[22] In this increasingly competitive world, no organization can sit back and relax. Continuous improvement is a way of life.

Confidentiality

Maintaining the confidentiality of buyer-seller relationships is always a concern. As suppliers become involved in design and they share ideas with buying organizations, both sides may fear that confidentiality may be compromised and that important information will leak to competitors, compromising the organizations' strategies or future plans. The ethical codes of all of the major purchasing professional organizations, including the Institute for Supply Management™, Purchasing Management Association of Canada, and the International Federation of Purchasing and Materials Management, stress the importance of honoring supplier confidentiality. Yet, the purchaser must ensure that he or she does not put the organization in a risky position, where the organization's proprietary information can be compromised.

Parameters for Disclosure

Regardless of the nature of the buyer-supplier relationship, the buyer and the supplier should sign mutual non-disclosure agreements. These agreements should be designed to protect both parties. The following is an example of a non-disclosure agreement included in a consulting contract:

> Consultant will not use or permit others to use, other than in connection with the work to be performed under this agreement, or disclose to third parties, any confidential information of Company X which is furnished to or otherwise acquired by Consultant in the course of its Work under this agreement or otherwise. All work standards, examples, or supplements are expected to be in full compliance of confidentiality agreements with all third parties.

If new products or services are being developed, the non-disclosure agreement may become more complex. It is critical to classify the expectations for rights of use and ownership upfront, in order to avoid potential conflicts, bad relationship outcomes, and even litigation.

Production Plan

It has become increasingly common for buying organizations to share production plans and schedules with suppliers. If this information is confidential in nature, a non-disclosure agreement should be signed. In addition, the buying organization should make it clear to its suppliers what their commitment is to the schedule. This should be by contract, so that the supplier knows, for instance, that the production schedule for the next two weeks is firm, that the two weeks beyond that is 50 percent firm, or the buyer would be liable for 50 percent of the inventory, and that beyond that there is no commitment. The contract is important, because if the buyer gives the supplier a schedule or plan, the supplier might not view it as a firm, written commitment, unless it is made clear through a legally binding agreement. This agreement protects both the buyer and the supplier, and clarifies obligations.

Product or Service Development

A concern that many organizations have relates to the idea of intellectual property. If the organization hires someone to come up with an idea, what if he or she takes that idea and gives it to someone else? What if the organization gives him or her access to some of its ideas and technology, and then he or she uses them elsewhere? There is no guaranteed way to avoid these risks, other than not allowing anyone to have access to proprietary ideas and technologies. If an organization is the best in any particular area, the wise approach might be to withhold information. That is the approach that Bose Corporation has taken with its sound technology, which the corporation sees as its core competence.[23] However, Bose does share and mutually develop ideas and technologies with its suppliers elsewhere. An organization must carefully weigh the risks and rewards of sharing information that could compromise its future viability if the information is disclosed.

Intellectual property agreements are not unusual. If an organization is paying someone for development work, his or her agreement might be as follows:

> Company X shall be the owner of any data, analysis, report, or work product generated by Contractor under this agreement. Contractor will promptly disclose to Company X any invention, discovery, trademark, copyrightable material, or commercial idea or plan arising from Contractor's work under this agreement. Company X will be or will be made the exclusive owner of any such invention, discovery and/or patent rights therein, trademark, copyrightable material and any copyright therein, or commercial idea or plan, and Contractor will execute such documents and take such other action at Company X's expense as may be necessary or appropriate to establish, register, or otherwise document Company X's ownership therein the United States and/or foreign countries.

Other agreements are also possible for specifying the sharing of rights and ownership, or for specifying exclusive rights for a given time period and shared rights after a given time period. The key is that these legally binding arrangements must be made in advance, or a disagreement is almost certain to follow when discoveries or new technologies are developed.

Almost all organizations have a policy of mutual protection of intellectual property rights. An example of the wording of one such policy is shown in the following:

Confidential information may include, but not be limited to, data, know-how, formulas, processes, designs, plans, specifications, samples, client lists, pricing information, sales policies, supplier lists, employee lists, and the like. With regard to any subsequent information which either party wishes to be treated as confidential, these items shall be clearly marked as confidential on all copies. Each party agrees to not disclose, without the express written permission of the other party, any confidential information and to treat such proprietary information as trade secrets.[24]

Non-disclosure and confidentiality agreements should be mutually beneficial, clarifying the expectations and rights of all parties concerned. This is becoming increasingly important as purchasers and suppliers work more closely in the early stages of design and development.

Key Points

1. It is critical for purchasing to be involved early in the design process to make a full contribution to a new product's or a new service's development.
2. Concurrent engineering is a manufacturing strategy that involves teams simultaneously developing the product and its supporting production processes. It is critical for purchasing to be involved in concurrent engineering.
3. Most of the costs of a product or service are incurred during the design phase.
4. Design for disassembly and design for the environment are methods that consider the life cycle implications of the product and service design process on the life cycle of the product or service.
5. Target costing is a valuable process that involves setting allowable costs for a new product or service during the design phase.
6. Speed to market is another important concept that reduces product/service development time and the actual product or service production and delivery time.

7. Early supplier involvement can reduce costs and cycle times and improve technology and service. Early supplier involvement is increasing in popularity as organizations realize its value.
8. Confidentiality of shared information is an important consideration in protecting the proprietary information and intellectual property of both parties. A legal agreement should be executed to clarify the expectations of both parties.

Questions for Review

1. Why is it critical for PSM to be involved in the design phase of products and/or services?
2. Briefly describe what is meant by "design for the environment" and the role that PSM can play in design for the environment?
3. What are some of the contributions that PSM can make to the target costing process?
4. Describe the difference between a white, gray, and black box approach to supplier involvement in design. When should each approach be applied?
5. What is the relevance of ESI to cycle time improvement?
6. How can buyers and suppliers protect the confidentiality of the information that they share with others?

For Additional Information

Burt, D.N. and R.L. Pinkerton. *Strategic Proactive Procurement*, AMACOM, New York, NY, 1996.

Dixon, L. and A. Porter-Millen. *JIT II: Revolution in Buying and Selling*, Cahners Publishing Company, Newton, MA, 1994.

Dowlatshahi, S. "Purchasing's Role in a Concurrent Engineering Environment," *International Journal of Purchasing and Materials Management*, (28: 1), Winter 1992, pp. 21-25.

Mendez, E. and J. Pearson. "Purchasing's Role in Product Development: The Case for Time Based Strategies," *International Journal of Purchasing and Materials Management*, (30: 1), Winter 1994, pp. 3-11.

Endnotes

1. Carter, C.R., T.E. Hendrick, and S.P. Siferd. "Purchasing's Involvement in Time-Based Strategies," *International Journal of Purchasing and Materials Management*, (32: 3), Summer 1996, pp. 2-10.
2. Fitzgerald, K.R. "Purchasing Unlocks Supply Treasures," *Purchasing Online*, March 11, 1999.
3. Dozbaba, M.S. "Financial Performance: Straight to the Bottom Line," *Purchasing Today*®, August 1998, pp. 18-21.
4. *Supplier Selection and Management Report*. IOMA, March 1996, www.lexisnexis.com.
5. Walton, S.V., R.B. Handfield, and S.A. Melnyk. "The Green Supply Chain: Integrating Suppliers into Environmental Management Processes," *International Journal of Purchasing and Materials Management*, (34: 2), pp. 2-11.
6. Florida, R. "Lean and Green: The Move to Environmentally Conscious Manufacturing," *California Management Review*, (39: 1), Fall 1996, pp. 80-105.
7. Maxwell, J., S. Rothenberg, F. Briscoe, and A. Marcus. "Green Schemes: Corporate Environmental Strategies and Their Implementation," *California Management Review*, (39: 3), Spring 1997, pp. 118-134.
8. Nelson, D., R. Mayo, and P.E. Moody. *Powered by Honda*, John Wiley and Sons, New York, NY, 1998, p. 106.
9. Zsidisin, G. and L.M. Ellram. "Supply Risk Assessment Analysis," *Practix: Best Practices in Purchasing and Supply Chain Management*, June 1999, pp. 9-12.
10. Zsidisin and Ellram, 1999.
11. Mazel, J. "What the Best-in-Class are Doing to Lower Their Material Acquisition Costs," *Supplier Selection and Management Report*, September 1999, p. 1.
12. *Supplier Selection and Management Report*. "Three Companies Reap Rewards from Early Supplier Involvement," March 1996, p. 1.
13. Stone, S. "DaimlerChrysler Uses One Global Supply Strategy," *Purchasing Online*, January 14, 1999.
14. *Tandem Journal*. "From Zero to 100 in 14 months," Third quarter 1999, pp. 14-16.

15. Ellram, L.M. *The Role of Supply Management in Target Costing*, Center for Advanced Purchasing Studies, Tempe, AZ, 1999.
16. Stalk, Jr., G. and T. Hout. *Time Based Competition*, video, Harvard Business School Videos, Boston, MA, 1993.
17. Fitzgerald, K.R. "Purchasing Unlocks Supply Treasures," *Purchasing Online*, March 11, 1999.
18. Minahan, T. "AlliedSignal Soars by Building Up Suppliers," *Purchasing*, September 18, 1997, pp. 38-47.
19. Stundza, T. "Seeking Tomorrow's Materials Today," *Purchasing*, February 12, 1998, p. 124.
20. Monckza, R., G. Ragatz, R.B. Handfield, R. Trent, and D. Frayer. "Executive Summary, Supplier Integration into New Product Development: A Strategy for Competitive Advantage," *The Global Procurement and Supply Chain Benchmarking Initiative*, Michigan State University, East Lansing, MI, 1997.
21. Minahan, 1997, pp. 43-44.
22. Minahan, 1997, pp. 44.
23. *JIT II: A Revolution in Buying and Selling*. Video, Bose Corporation, Framingham, MA, 1994.
24. Grieco, M. "Can I Tell You a Secret?" *Purchasing Today*®, December 1999, p. 20.

CHAPTER 7

PLANNING AND DEVELOPING SOURCING STRATEGY BASED ON FORECAST DATA

How can purchasing and supply management integrate its knowledge of markets and strategies to achieve the best results?

Chapter Objectives

- To understand the purpose of forecasting and purchasing and supply management's role in the forecasting process
- To be aware of key economic issues that shape and affect forecasting
- To comprehend forecasting terminology
- To be cognizant of the key sources of forecast data
- To become familiar with the major forecasting methodologies
- To appreciate the many factors that affect forecasts

Introduction

A forecast is a prediction of the future. Forecasting can examine a variety of issues, from broad issues such as trends in global trade, inflation, and spending power, to very specific issues such as population trends in a given market over the next several months. Forecasting of macro-level economic, industry, and competitive issues and trends feeds into the organization's high-level strategic plans. Micro-level forecasting of details, such as the demand of a specific customer for a specific week, becomes part of the organization's operating plan. Forecasting is the primary means to match external customer demands and market conditions with the capabilities and capacity of the organization. Forecasting is critical because it drives the organization's behavior, including the level of the workforce to retain; the need for production and distribution facilities and equipment; transportation needs; and, of course, the raw materials, components, and supplies needs. The planning process is dealt with in depth in volume four of this series, *The Supply Management Leadership Process.*

Purchasing and supply management is considered a boundary-spanning function in that it interacts directly with people within the organization and outside of the organization. Through its interaction with suppliers and the marketplace, purchasing and supply management gains intelligence about trends, new technologies, product availability, labor shortages, and other issues. The information gathered can be very useful to the organization for developing plans, formulating strategies, and, at a tactical level, determining the most favorable types of contractual arrangements with suppliers. Thus, in order to be effective, the purchasing and supply management function plays a critical role as both a provider and a recipient of forecast data.

This chapter introduces the purpose of forecasting. Key economic issues and data that support forecasting are presented, as well as definitions of some specific terms that are frequently used in forecasting. Some major sources of forecast data are also described. The chapter closes with a brief description of major forecasting techniques and explains some of the factors that can affect forecast accuracy.

Reasons for Forecasting

If the world were a static place, there would be no need to forecast. Everyone would always know what was going to happen next. How boring life would be! Fortunately, the world is dynamic and constantly changing, changing too fast for many people. As Michael Porter pointed out in his seminal work on corporate strategy, there are five forces that shape industry competition:

- The threat of potential entrants
- The supply market
- The potential for substitution of the product/service sold by the company
- The buyers in the marketplace
- The actions taken by competitors[1]

These forces, as well as other factors presented later in this chapter, pose potential threats that the organization needs to monitor. When possible, the organization should forecast trends in the future direction and include the likely market impact of potential threats and opportunities.

Types of Forecasts

The type of forecast needed varies based on the reason for the forecast, the nature of the item or trend being forecast, and the time horizon of the forecast. *Fact-based* forecasts use historical information, such as price or production data, to project future trends. This type of forecast often uses detailed information to generate specific forecasts. *Opinion-based* forecasts use expert judgments to estimate future events, such as the impact of technology on a particular industry in the next 10 years. Another type of forecast, called a *change index*, is finding increasing use, and it is the format of the ISM *Report On Business*®. This type of forecast is excellent for looking at major trends or shifts in the environment.

To purchasing and supply managers, the ability to forecast required quantities, material availability, and prices represents a competitive and strategic advantage. With the realities of global markets come the need to study and forecast commodity and industry changes based on worldwide commodity and industry trends. Thus, while purchasing and supply management tends to be interested in specific data to use in operations, purchasing managers often use macro data as a basis for predicting specific trends.

Major Concerns for Purchasing and Supply Management in Forecasting

Quantity – This is an immediate concern for most purchasers. Questions to ask include: How much of an item should I purchase or contract for in order to meet the organization's needs on a timely basis, without creating excessive inventory? When should I buy to get the best price? How can I be sure the item will be available when I need it? If purchasers do not have forecasts of requirements for purchased goods and services, they risk buying the wrong quantities.

Forecasts for items to be used to produce a good or service are based on sales projections, including seasonal and cyclical issues.

Industry Capacity and Availability – Forecasts of availability in the short and long term also help purchasers determine when to buy and how much to buy. These forecasts are based on commodity studies that examine the worldwide supply and demand, including sources of supply; reserves; and the effect of technological change on the manufacturing process, uses, and demand. These forecasts are often available from industry associations. Some companies, such as Cargill and M & M Mars, have economists on staff to keep tabs on shifts in the key markets in which they participate as buyers or suppliers.

Cost or Price – Price levels should also be forecast, especially for purchasing, which tends to have accountability for price variance. Many factors, beyond simple supply and demand, determine price. These factors include the five forces mentioned previously; the influences of governmental action; and laws and regulations affecting labor, hazardous commodities, utilities, and other issues. Perceptions of supply shortages, such as those caused by the threat of a war or a strike, may also affect prices. In any forecasting exercise, the potential market influences on cost or price projections must be considered.

Technology – Technological changes are a significant factor in many markets. Purchasers do not want to lock their employers into long-term contracts when technology is rapidly changing. This is particularly true in the areas of information technology and telecommunications, where changes are continual. Yesterday's favorite technology can be purchased today at a deep discount, if the organization still wants it. Forecasting technological shifts has become a major pastime for organizations such as GartnerGroup, which forecasts trends in information technology industries. Member companies pay a fee for the latest update. While such memberships may be expensive, the cost of ignoring rapid change is even more expensive. Thus, companies in high-technology industries, or those that spend a great deal on high-technology purchases, must forecast both the timing of the technological changes and which of the competing technologies will be the winner.

Planning – Many facets of organizational planning and budgeting depend on the flow of accurate information about the supply markets. Examples include decisions to build or expand capacity, the ability to fulfill sales projections, investment choices between new or existing technologies, and decisions on whether to enter certain markets.

Ensuring supply – The ability to meet supply needs on a timely basis can make the difference between lost sales and a highly profitable product. A recent *Practix* study profiled a high-technology company with a strong focus on managing any "event that could disrupt production."[2] The organization has a sophisticated risk-assessment process that considers the availability of the item purchased as a key criterion. Within the risk factor of availability, supplier lead-times, future technological capability, and volume capacity must be forecast.

General Economic Issues in Forecasting

This section presents an overview of the U.S. economy, global markets, and many of the trends and issues that affect forecasting.

The U.S. Economy

The economy of the United States has developed into five separate economies. Each of these economies has its own behavior, and it reacts differently to economic change. Each is tracked separately for forecasting purposes. The five separate economies are summarized in the following:

Old-Line Industry – This sector is made up of the basic manufacturing industries, such as autos, steel, machinery, textiles, and appliances. This sector faces strong international competition, as well as major restructuring and investment problems.

Energy – The energy sector includes the natural resources, technology, and facilities used to meet energy needs. This sector faces worldwide scarcity and powerful cartels. Major investment problems exist in this sector.

High-Technology – This sector includes firms that manufacture semiconductors, computers, and industrial and home electronics. Currently, this sector has tremendous growth potential, as well as volatility and rapid change.

Agriculture – The "foodstuffs" industry includes growers, packers, and distributors. World demand in this sector is experiencing spotty growth. Productivity is high, but it is beginning to decline.

Services – This is the fastest-growing sector. It includes health services, financial services, personal services, communications and information services, and entertainment. This sector is attracting a great deal of capital, is growing around the world, and is gaining in productivity.

In a free-market economy, price is generally determined by supply and demand. In a socialistic economy, price is determined by a central administration. But even in a free-enterprise, capitalistic economy, prices sometimes bear little relationship to supply and demand. A price can be set by regulation, as were electric utility prices prior to deregulation in the late 1990s and early 2000s.

The only situations that are close to perfect competition are some commodity markets that are operated on open exchanges, such as the Grain Exchange in Minneapolis. Similarly, with the advent of deregulation, there is no such thing as a complete monopoly. Most market situations fall somewhere between perfect competition and monopoly; they are in a condition of imperfect competition in which each supplier has some control over its own prices. A limited number of rivals exist in each market, power shifts occur over time among buyers and suppliers, and products can usually be differentiated in some way. An example of this comes from the retail consumer products sectors. In the late 1970s and early 1980s, major consumer goods companies, such as Procter and Gamble, had power over their suppliers. Today, the tables have turned, and Procter and Gamble's suppliers, companies such as Wal-Mart, have more power in the channel, and they dictate terms and policies to Procter and Gamble.[3]

The Nature of Demand

Supply and demand are said to have *elasticity*, meaning that they respond to changes in price in the marketplace. The elasticity of demand is defined by what happens to total revenue as price is cut. Demand is said to be *elastic* when a reduction in price increases total revenue, so that the increase in quantity purchased more than offsets the lower unit price. Demand is *inelastic* if a reduction in price results in lower total revenue, meaning that people don't buy enough additional units to offset the revenue impact of the lower price. Demand is referred to as *unitary elastic* when a reduction in price does not change total revenue. Elasticity of supply, on the other hand, measures the responsiveness of producers to the quantities they are willing to make available as price changes.

The purchasing professional needs to consider the elasticity of supply and demand as the availability of goods fluctuates, and as firms and plants adjust to new levels of demand. The total demand for a product is represented by the sum of the "wants" of all buyers. Buyers differ considerably. Some have more money to spend, or have a greater need for the product or service. When all of the individual demands at each price are added together, the result is referred to as the market demand curve. This demand curve shifts as the amount of money available to buyers changes. As successive units of the product are produced, the extra utility added by the last unit tends to decrease — this is known as the Law of Diminishing Marginal Utility. Utility can be thought of as satisfaction derived from the item — how important or valuable a unit of the product is to a buyer. This relationship is shown in Figure 7.1A.

Likewise, the total supply of a product is represented by the sum of the supply curves of all the independent producers of the item. The aggregate is the industry's supply curve. The slope of this curve reflects the cost to produce the good. The marginal cost at any output level is the additional cost of producing one extra unit. The marginal cost curve is a rising curve because of the Law of Diminishing Returns. If an organization obtains diminishing returns from a factor of production, the organization also has increasing marginal cost. This relationship is shown in Figure 7.1B.

Most companies are interested in maximizing their profits in the long run, and therefore, they will continue to produce only if prices at least cover expenses. They will produce less if prices are low, and they will produce more if prices are high. When an organization produces at a market price that just covers its variable costs, it will be on the verge of shutting down. At higher prices, the company will obtain revenue to help cover its fixed costs, and at still higher prices, it will make a profit. Therefore, the ideal competitive market condition in an industry is one in which the willingness of buyers to pay, and the actual minimized marginal costs of the producers, are in reasonable balance. If a balance is not achieved, the market will experience volatile fluctuations in price and supply, as players enter and leave the market based on its current pricing structure.

FIGURE 7.1
Law of Diminishing Marginal Utility and
Law of Diminishing Returns

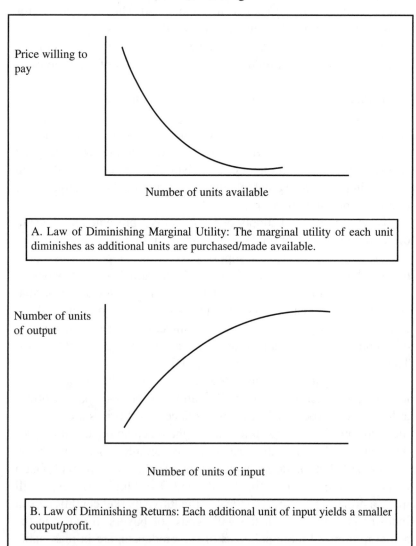

A. Law of Diminishing Marginal Utility: The marginal utility of each unit diminishes as additional units are purchased/made available.

B. Law of Diminishing Returns: Each additional unit of input yields a smaller output/profit.

Global Markets

The U.S. economy is a vital part of the growing world economy. Just as countries throughout the world felt the economic impact of the Asian financial crisis from 1997 to 1998, trends and developments throughout all of the industrialized nations have a significant impact on the global economy. The scope and composition of international trade are continually changing; sources, prices, and conditions of sale and payment shift continuously.

Many nations hold economic advantages in certain commodity areas. Saudi Arabia, for instance, has oil; Canada has timber; Zimbabwe has chrome. Other countries have advantages in labor supply, location, or climate. An absolute advantage in international trade exists when one of the trading countries can produce a unit of the good with less resources than the other countries, or when only one country has a resource (such as South Africa with its natural industrial diamonds).

From a global economic perspective, the concept of *comparative advantage* is more important. A nation has a comparative advantage when it is more efficient than other nations in producing the same good.[4] On this basis, a country will specialize in exporting the products for which it holds a comparative advantage. However, as history has shown, comparative advantage can be fleeting. Companies flocked to Japan to take advantage of low labor costs in the 1970s and early 1980s, then to Hong Kong, Taiwan, Korea, and now China. Unless it is based on natural resources, a comparative advantage can be temporary.

The natural flow of world trade, which reflects whatever advantages exist, is modified by many factors. Embargoes and quotas can stop or slow the flow of goods, tariffs can wash out price differences, and government subsidies can create artificial comparative advantages where none exist. In some cases, goods are exported at prices below their production costs. This practice, called *dumping*, is becoming increasingly common in international trade. In parts of the developing world, government owned and operated companies will sell products for export below variable cost. The government would have to pay the employees whether they worked or not, so if even a portion of the labor cost and all of the other variable costs are covered, the government comes out ahead. This type of strategy is a short-term approach, which will eventually lead to substantial price increases.

Business Cycles and Trends

The level of national income and production fluctuates because earnings, consumption levels, savings, production, employment, profits, and so forth are constantly changing. All business cycles differ in intensity and duration. A *recession* is a downturn in economic activity, whereas an *expansion* represents an upward trend in economic indicators. Overlaid on this pattern are long-term economic trends and seasonal variations.

Many factors contribute to the cyclical pattern. Political disturbances, wars, population migrations, natural disasters, weather conditions, and governmental actions in monetary and fiscal policy affect the economy.

Economic Indicators

The Bureau of Economic Analysis (BEA) of the U.S. Department of Commerce has identified and classified key indicators of economic trends based on their tendency to turn or change direction before, during, or after the general economy's cycles. *Leading indicators* change direction before the turning point of the general economy, *lagging indicators* follow the economy, and *coincident indicators* turn with the economy. The BEA forms these groups of indicators into composite indices. Leading indicators are thought to represent the future expectations of business, in general, toward product demand, labor, and financial markets. Lagging indicators reflect the costs of past consumption and activities, and therefore, they lag behind general economic changes. Coincident indicators reflect the current economic conditions. A summary of how the various indicators are grouped is shown in Table 7.1.

Business cycle forecasting models rely on leading indicators, such as average hours worked per week, stock prices, construction contract awards, and new orders. Some models provide fair estimates of expected changes in the gross national product (GNP). Purchasing and inventory management decisions can be made using this information.

TABLE 7.1
Key Economic Indicators

Leading Indicators

Average weekly hours of production workers
Manufacturers' new orders for consumer goods
Manufacturers' unfilled orders for durable goods
Orders for new plants and equipment
Producer Price Index
Supplier leadtime performance
Average weekly new claims for unemployment
Index of Consumer Expectations
Stock prices of 500 common stocks
Housing starts
Amount of money in circulation

Lagging Indicators

Consumer Price Index
Average bank prime interest rate
Volume of outstanding business loans
Ratio of consumer installment credit to personal income
Index of manufacturing labor cost per unit of output
Manufacturing inventory/sales ratio
Average unemployment duration

Coincident Indicators

Industrial Production Index
Manufacturing and trade sales
Non-agricultural employment
Personal income net of transfer payments

Key Indicators

Money Supply – As a leading indicator, money supply refers to the total of a nation's money available for spending. It consists of currency and bank deposits held by private businesses and individuals. There are three commonly used measures of the money supply. The first measure, M-1, is made up of currency plus demand deposits. The second measure, M-2, consists of M-1 plus time deposit balances (savings accounts). The third measure, M-3, incorporates M-2 plus time deposits (such as certificates of deposit) held at commercial banks and savings banks. Economists keep track of M-1, M-2, and M-3, as well as other measures of the money supply, to better understand the direction of the economy.

Interest Rates – These are a lagging indicator, and they refer to the price paid for borrowing money. Interest rates vary based on factors that include the lender's willingness to postpone use of the money, the lender's willingness to assume the loaning funds, the possibility that economic changes will reduce the purchasing power of the funds by the time they are repaid, and the administrative costs of processing a loan. Interest rates also depend on the market for a particular loan (that is, the demand for a loan by the borrowers, and the supply of funds available for such lending).

Inflation – The relevance of inflation to purchasing managers is great, because this economic factor creates a loss of purchasing power when prices increase for needed items. Inflation is not an indicator used in the BEA's composite indexes. However, anticipated price increases encourage purchasing managers to place orders promptly, a practice that tends to exacerbate inflation. Purchasing becomes more complex during inflationary periods because reorder quantity calculations need to be modified to reflect prospective price increases. Inflation represents a change in the level of average prices in the economy. The United States has experienced inflation of 2 to 9 percent per year since the 1930s.

Level of Unemployment – This leading indicator is represented as a percentage of the labor force that is unemployed. Typically, about 4 percent of the labor force will be unemployed. Therefore, "full employment" means about 96 percent employment. The United States was at about full employment in the late 1990s and the early 2000s. Under the Employment Act of 1946, the government was charged with ensuring full employment. Through fiscal policy, set by Congress, the government shapes taxation and public spending to dampen the swings of the business cycle and to maintain high employment. Monetary policy, under the Federal Reserve Board, also plays a role by shaping consumption and savings. The two together represent the government's power to influence the economy.

Trade and Exchange Rates – These rates determine how much a buying firm will owe another firm based in a foreign country. Historically, exchange rates were determined under the gold standard, with each national currency converted into a specified amount of gold. When the gold standard was abandoned, the trading nations adopted a system of fixed exchange rates. Today, some foreign exchange rates "float" between parameters established by the central banks. Others are "fixed" by the central banks, and they are adjusted only for major economic changes. For example, the countries using the Euro (EU) all have a fixed exchange rate to the EU. Thus, within certain parameters, exchange rates respond to the market and to economic activity. While each country desires its currency to be "strong" relative to that of its trading partners, it doesn't want its currency to be too strong. For example, when the U.S. dollar is too strong, it is more difficult to sell U.S. products abroad, because it takes more foreign currency to pay for U.S. products. Also, too strong of a dollar reduces domestic investment, because the dollar goes further in overseas investments.

Balance of Trade and Payments – This refers to the balance of merchandise trade between nations. The balance for the United States is favorable if the nation exports more merchandise than it imports. When the balance of merchandise account is added to other accounts, such as tourist spending and foreign investment, a "balance of payments" is created. The United States has been in an unfavorable trade and payments position since 1950.

Gross Domestic Product (GDP) – This indicator approximates the former GNP. The GDP represents the final consumption of all goods and services in the economy and is a general measure of economic activity. Note that the GDP measures final goods and services, hence these are purchases by households and government, but not those of industry. There are various components within GDP measuring activities that seek to adjust for depreciation, taxes, and savings rates.

Governmental Policies

Government is in the unique position to have an impact on economic activity. Through various means solely at its disposal, government can influence the economic behavior of individuals and organizations. In addition to the means mentioned previously, the following policies affect economic activity:

Fiscal Policy – This is the government's ability to spend and tax. For example, economic activity can be stimulated when the U.S. Army Corps of Engineers performs public works projects without a government tax increase. The government can also lower tax rates to increase the money supply and encourage consumer spending, or raise tax rates to slow spending.

Monetary Policy – Government uses monetary policy to adjust the amount of money in circulation. The quantity of money relative to the demand for its use drives interest rates higher or lower. This mechanism is handled by the Federal Reserve, which buys government securities to add liquidity and sells bonds to reduce it.

Budget Deficits – Deficits were common in the United States from the mid-1960s through the late 1990s. The deficits were reversed with the tremendous, sustained economic growth in the late 1990s. Budget deficits affect monetary policy. The government's need for borrowed money and the rates of interest that result compete with industry's need for capital to finance new plants and equipment. Thus, deficits reduce the economy's growth potential and its competitiveness in markets both at home and abroad.

Other Global Economic Issues

Political Stability/Instability – A foreign country's political stability should be carefully considered before doing business with that country. This is not only true in Third World countries, but also in developed countries such as Australia and Norway, where heavily unionized populations, transportation strikes, and plant and port closings are not unusual. The worst case scenario would be nationalization, in which the government of the country seizes the company's assets and asks the company to leave the country.

World Industrial Migration – This migration has been accelerating since the late 1960s. Differences between countries in labor, inflation, interest rates, and currency rates have caused shifts in manufacturing throughout the world. Increasingly, firms are moving to less developed countries to tap local markets for their low production costs as well as their sales outlets to emerging economies.

Free Trade and Protectionism – Free trade refers to a no-barrier situation, in which there are no tariffs, no quotas, and no embargoes on trade. The term *fair trade* usually implies protectionism, which means selective and graduated tariffs and carefully negotiated quotas on selected products (for instance, quotas on the number of canvas shoes imported). Protectionist measures are also instituted for government buying, particularly Department of Defense (DOD) buying. In the case of the DOD, protectionism is instituted on the grounds of national security.

Most economists agree that protectionism is not in the country's long-range interest, and not in the interest of a healthy world economy. This has been the impetus for the emergence of the European Economic Community (EEC), the North American Free Trade Agreement (NAFTA), and other agreements throughout the world.

Countertrade – In this type of protectionist measure, a country requires that foreign companies doing business in that country also export goods from that country. Countertrade encourages money to flow both ways, and it is useful when the foreign country's currency is not easily converted in the world market or when the country does not possess the currency to pay for such purchases. For example, barter occurs when one firm swaps its goods with another organization, accepting the goods as another form of payment. Such arrangements may take place because of a lack of trading currency, but the difficulty lies in matching buyers and suppliers.

In contrast, offset trade usually occurs with government involvement, especially when government purchases are at stake. Military purchases may be most common, where a nation agrees to purchase new weapons from an industry in country X provided the selling country purchases a like amount of product from it. The outcome is that the balance of payments for the buying nation is not adversely impacted by the military purchase.

Environmental Concerns – Regulations vary significantly by country (and even by state within the United States), and they may make it more or less attractive to do business in a certain country. For example, Germany has some of the toughest environmental laws in the world. As Germany's laws get tougher, costs may increase. It is important for organizations conducting business in other countries and regions to be familiar with current and pending environmental legislation that may affect the cost and complexity of future business transactions.

Economic Terms and Concepts in Forecasting

This chapter has already introduced some of the basic terminology of economics. This section introduces additional concepts that are relevant to purchasing and supply management in both developing and using forecast data.

Indexing

Economic indexing is a common approach for comparing a figure from a base period to a figure from a later period. Indexing summarizes and examines changes in the direction or level of economic activity. Index numbers relate such things as annual industrial production, industrial prices, and consumer prices to those of base years.

At the time an index is established, a base period or year is defined with an index of 100. The base year is often selected as a period when the economy is relatively stable, without high inflation, recession, or high unemployment. All other comparison years or periods are represented as percentage differences from that base year or period. For example, if 1992 were the base year (100) for a particular statistic, and the 1995 index number for that activity were 105, then the economic activity in 1995 would be 5 percent greater than the base period.

The formula for calculating percent changes between two periods is:

index for current period of interest / index for prior period of interest * 100

For example, if 2000 had an index number of 130, then comparing 2000 to 1995 would get:

130 / 105 * 100 = 123.8

Thus, the year 2000 is 23.8 percent higher than 1995, in terms of 1992 (base year) units.

Price Indices

Price indices are a common measure of economic change. A comparison of prices in one year to a base year yields a price index. The best-known price indices in the United States are the Producer Price Index, the Consumer Price Index, and the GDP deflator or Implicit Price Deflator. These indices measure the percentage change in prices compared to a base year.

Producer Price Index (PPI) – The PPI is reported each month by the Bureau of Labor Statistics(BLS) of the U.S. Department of Labor. These data are published around the middle of the month following the month to which they refer, and the information is available online at www.bls.gov. The three PPIs are for finished goods; intermediate materials, supplies, and components; and raw materials. The BLS Web site provides a great deal of specific information about commodities, and it is worth browsing to get a feel for trends. These three indices are also consolidated into the "all commodities" index. Prices used in these indices represent the actual producer transaction prices, and are seasonally adjusted.

Consumer Price Index (CPI) – The CPI gauges the overall rate of change for a fixed basket of household goods and services. The BLS generates this index, which is published toward the end of the month following the month to which it refers. Again, this information is available online at the BLS Web site. Approximately every 10 years, the "basket" is revised to reflect changes in consumer tastes and purchases. Food, beverages, housing, education, medical care, transportation, apparel, and entertainment are among the items measured by this index. The CPI is a measure of urban population purchases only, and it excludes rural household purchases, as well as those of military personnel and persons in institutional settings, such as prisons, homes for the aged, and long-term hospital care. Like the PPI, the CPI is seasonally adjusted. The CPI is not a good measure for businesses, because it includes a mix of consumer spending and is heavily skewed by the impact of housing costs.

Implicit Price Deflator – Also known as the GDP deflator, this index is used by the Department of Commerce to compare the average level of prices in one year to those of a base year (1982). This index includes the effect on overall price of changes in the distribution of goods and services bought in the marketplace. The Implicit Price Deflator is calculated by dividing current-dollar (or nominal) GDP by constant-dollar GDP (real GDP, which has been deflated for price increases since the base year). It is used as an overall measure of inflation in the economy.

Interest Rates

Interest is the term for the cost of borrowing money. An interest rate is generally expressed as the annual percentage of the principal that the borrower must pay for the use of borrowed funds. Interest rates vary depending on perceived repayment risk, duration of loan, and inflation expectations. Among the well-known measures of short-, medium-, and long-term interest rates are the following: U.S. Treasury three-month bills, U.S. Treasury notes and bonds with maturities between three and 10 years, high-grade municipal bonds, corporate AAA bonds, Federal Reserve discount rate, prime rate charged by commercial banks, and new home mortgage rates. Information regarding these rates is available in *The Wall Street Journal* and the business sections of most newspapers.

As mentioned previously, the Federal Reserve Board's discount rate is part of the government's monetary policy. It is closely watched and generally has a significant impact on all of the other interest rates listed above. High interest rates promote saving and repayment of loans. Low interest rates, as experienced in the United States throughout the 1950s, 1960s, and 1990s, encourage spending, borrowing, and economic growth. Interest rates reflect the general expectations of future economic conditions.

Capacity Utilization

The Federal Reserve Board also issues a monthly report that calculates capacity utilization in the manufacturing, mining, and electric and gas utilities industries. This index represents the ratio of the Industrial Production Index to plant and equipment capacity. These figures are seasonally adjusted. This is an inferential statistic that is derived from year-end surveys conducted by several governmental and private organizations. The survey information is used to assess the current fitness and trends in each of the industries. High utilization indicates a robust economy, while low utilization shows weakness.

Data Sources Used in Forecasting

Every fact-based or quantitative forecast begins with data gathering. There are numerous sources of relevant, useful information, including external data such as governmental data and forecasts, private company or organization forecasts, commercial forecasts (made available to subscribers), and internal company data and forecasts.

ISM *Report On Business* (Manufacturing and Non-Manufacturing)

The ISM *Report On Business*® is one of the most widely watched and highly regarded of all the leading economic indicators. Developed in the 1940s, it is regularly mentioned on television and radio in the national business news and cited in *The Wall Street Journal*, *The New York Times*, and other publications. The ISM *Report On Business*® is derived from a poll of approximately 400 companies in 20 manufacturing industries from around the country. Unlike other business system indicators, the ISM *Report On Business*® does not measure the level of activity, but the change in level of activity. The purchasing managers surveyed are asked to report changes from the previous month for production, new orders, supplier deliveries, inventories, employment, and commodity prices. Purchasing managers report whether each activity was "higher/better than," "the same as," or "less/worse than" the previous month. For each of these indicators, a "diffusion index" is formed by adding all of the "higher/better" responses together with half of the "same" responses to develop the indicator. ISM then seasonally adjusts this total to arrive at the final index number.

The report has two specific advantages. First, upward or downward turns in diffusion indices have the property of leading upward or downward turns in the actual activities. A recent study found that the ISM indices generally lead the business cycle turning points.[5] Second, unlike governmental data, which is often several months old when it is released, the ISM data describe changes in the previous month's activity. The data are typically no more than a week to 10 days old. For these reasons, the ISM *Report On Business*® is extremely valuable as a forecasting tool.

In 1998, ISM launched the Non-Manufacturing ISM *Report On Business®* in response to the growing economic activity in the service sector. The report is based on monthly surveys of more than 370 purchasing and supply management professionals in the non-manufacturing sector. Questions examine business activity, new orders, backlog of orders, new export orders, inventory change, inventory sentiment, imports, prices, employment, and supplier deliveries. The respondents represent agriculture, forestry, and fisheries; mining; construction; transportation, communications, electric, gas, and sanitary services; wholesale trade; retail trade; finance, insurance, and real estate; services; and public administration. This report is a valuable tool for forecasting service sector trends.

In addition to the national ISM *Report On Business®*, many local ISM affiliates — including the Purchasing Management Associations in Arizona, Austin, Boston, Buffalo, Chicago, Cincinnati, Cleveland, Detroit, Milwaukee, Oregon, Rock River Valley, South Bend, Southwestern Michigan, Toledo, and Washington — publish their own regional business surveys. These surveys, which are similar to the ISM *Report On Business®* in methodology, reflect local or regional situations that may differ significantly from the national conditions.

Government Publications

One of the primary sources of external data is the government: federal, state, and local governmental agencies gather and publish a tremendous amount of valuable information, most available free or at very low cost. There is also an increasing amount of data available online. The Bureau of Labor Statistics (www.bls.gov), the Bureau of Economic Analysis (www.bea.doc.gov), and the Bureau of the Census (www.census.gov) all have rich Web sites, with links to many additional valuable sites. New data are added to these sites regularly. In addition, most metropolitan areas have libraries that are designated as federal repositories, which contain information disseminated by the federal government. Some of the more useful documents for purchasing managers are mentioned in the following:

Survey of Current Business – This monthly publication is from the Bureau of Economic Analysis of the U.S. Department of Commerce. It provides estimates and analysis of U.S. economic activity, including useful indicator data, business statistics, reviews of current economic developments, and quarterly national income and gross domestic product figures.

Federal Reserve Bulletin – This monthly bulletin prepared by the Federal Reserve Board contains information on monetary policy as well as financial statistics, such as flow of funds measures, interest rates, savings, wages, and prices.

Business Conditions Digest – This publication examines leading, coincident, and lagging economic indicators.

Economic Report of the President – This publication forecasts the economic outlook for the next year and presents goals related to monetary and fiscal policy.

Statistical Abstract of the U.S. – The abstract contains a wealth of information on employment, income, population, and vital statistics for all major sectors of the economy. The economic information includes imports, exports, price trends, industry employment, wages, and overtime, which are of particular interest to purchasing managers.

These represent only a few of the many sources of data available from the federal government. Go online to one of the sites mentioned previously to see other accessible data.

Each year the United Nations publishes global information that is applicable to purchasing and materials management forecasting needs, including "International Trade Statistics," "World Economic Survey," and "Statistics of World Trade in Steel."

Private Publications

In addition to the ISM *Report On Business*®, many other professional associations such as the American Production and Inventory Control Society (APICS), industry associations, and special interest groups publish surveys or analyses of economic conditions for their members. Business forecasts can be found in *APICS, P&IM Review* (for example, the inventory-to-sales ratio), and *Electronic Buyer's News* (for example, the Quest Index). *Purchasing* magazine publishes commodity price trends regularly in "Buylines," and the magazine even hosts a contest for forecasting. It also has a monthly and online feature called "Buying News," which offers prices, forecasts, and articles on metals; chemicals; electronics; transport and logistics;

automotive; original equipment manufacturer (OEM) parts; energy; plastics; computers; office products; and maintenance, repair and operating (MRO) supplies. In addition, many industry associations, such as those serving the chemical industry, maintain Web sites that feature current pricing data and forecasts.

Commercial Forecasts

Many organizations develop and market economic forecasts for sale to subscribers. Some are available via paper subscriptions, but an increasing number are available online. Among those offering forecasts for a fee are banks and industry groups. There are forecasts for subscribers for everything from pulp and paper to PCs to manure. Customized forecasts are available from many of these firms. Some Internet sites, such as the chemical industry site, give users the option to pay for and receive specific commodity forecasts online.

Internal Historical Data

Internal historical data can be useful for forecasting the demand for a product to a specific level, such as a stock-keeping unit (sku) in retail, or the demand for a particular service in a service industry, such as an auto repair shop. For example, forecasts of sales for individual products and families of products can be determined by using internal records to understand seasonal and cyclical demand patterns, the impact of new product introductions, leadtimes, and the impact of special pricing offers. Many organizations now have historical data available on their intranets, so it is no longer necessary to spend hours gathering such data.

Forecasting Methodologies/Techniques

This section discusses some of the major issues associated with forecasting as well as several of the more important forecasting methods.

Forecasting Levels

Forecasts can be near-term or long-term, and they can look at broad or specific issues. The level of forecasting that is appropriate depends on the purpose of the forecast. Determining whether to use long- or short-term data and macro- or micro-level detail is a first step in the forecasting process.

Short-Term vs. Long-Term Forecasting – A short-term forecast is used as an aid in developing and executing short-term purchase plans and operational or tactical activities. A short-term forecast can look at what is needed in the next day to what is needed as far out as a year. The nearer the term, the more detailed and accurate the forecast must be, because specific production schedules are being planned and materials are being purchased. For example, when a company like Pillsbury forecasts its volume for refrigerated biscuits, it forecasts the total refrigerated biscuit volume for the three- to five-year period. For the next year, it forecasts volume by product family, such as dinner rolls, Hungry Jack products, and so on. As the year approaches, it begins to forecast volume by item and flavor, such as Hungry Jack Flaky 10-count, providing enough detail for the proper ordering of ingredients and packaging, and for production planning. Each Pillsbury division uses *macro-forecast information*, such as projected gross domestic product or industry growth data. Macro-forecasts project broad sales activities. These data may be developed by internal experts or come from external sources, such as the government.

Based on macro-forecasts and strategic plans, each division also develops micro-forecasts, which are specific to the organization or limited to specific, relevant aspects of larger issues. The linkage occurs when an organization forecasts specific commodity prices for the next year (micro), which depend on projections of global supply market conditions (macro). The organization's projection for the next year's inventory level (micro) is based on sales estimates, which, in turn, are based on general economic condition forecasts (macro).

With the advent of e-commerce, increased use of bar coding, and improved information sharing among suppliers and customers, some organizations no longer need to create short-term forecasts. They use actual customer sales or usage figures to create production schedules. An example of this is Campbell's Soup. It receives daily electronic updates from its customers, informing Campbell's of their demand for all Campbell's products, as well as their warehouse inventory levels.[6] Of course, Campbell's must still plan for the longer term, but it no longer has to deal with the costs and complexities of short-term forecast errors.

Demand Patterns in Forecast Data

There is no point in forecasting if the data used are totally random and cannot be predicted in any way. Data have a tendency to follow patterns. The art of forecasting is the ability to identify the patterns that underlie the data, and then use those patterns to assess potential future demand. The most common way to display data is in a tabular format, which presents data in organized lists or tables. This makes it easy to show precise numbers. Graphs are an excellent tool to illustrate trends and patterns in data.

Central Tendency – This measure helps to provide a perspective for the middle range of the data. Measures of central tendency include the mean, mode, and median. The mean is the average of all the values in the set. The mode is the most frequently appearing value in the set. The median is the midpoint, when the set is arranged from lowest to highest value.

Variability – This measure shows how the data are dispersed. The smaller the measure of variability, the more tightly the numbers cluster around the central point. Measures of variability include the range, variance, and standard deviation. The range of a set of numbers is the largest number minus the smallest. The variance equals the squared sum of the differences of the individual values of a set from the mean, divided by the number of values in the set. The standard deviation is the square root of the variance.

Analysis of Cyclical Data – This analysis uncovers a cycle, or the residual variation fluctuating around the long-term trend, such as changes in the economic or business system. Seasonal variations occur annually on a repetitive basis. Seasonal, as well as economic, cycles can make the detection of long-term trends difficult. For this reason, data are often seasonally adjusted, which means that the cyclical component of the data is removed. For example, in developing a forecast, a purchaser may want to remove snowmobile sales for a year in which there was little snow. The objective is to uncover the long-range, underlying trend in the data. Is the snowmobile sales decrease due to the fact that there was no snow last year, or is some of the decrease attributable to a sustainable long-term decrease in demand?

Trend Analysis – This analysis attempts to uncover the long-term direction of a series of data. Factors that produce trends or trend changes include population changes, productivity changes, technology changes, supply/demand changes, and price changes. In the case of snowmobiles, changes in global climatic conditions and stricter laws could have a long-term impact on sales.

Forecast Methods

Once the required level of forecast data and underlying patterns have been determined, the proper forecast technique can be chosen. Some of the popular types of forecast methods are presented in the following sections. Qualitative forecasts are useful where little historic data is available, or when the historic data are irrelevant. Qualitative forecasts rely on expert opinions. Quantitative techniques use past data to predict the future. The major forecast methods are summarized in Table 7.2.

TABLE 7.2
Key Forecast Methods

Forecast Category	Types of Forecasts
Qualitative	○ Delphi ● Expert Opinion ● Intuition
Quantitative —Causal Modeling	○ Regression ● Correlation
—Time Series Analysis	○ Moving Average ● Weighted Moving Average ● Exponential Smoothing
Mix of Quantitative and Qualitative —Market Research	○ Test Market ● Consumer Surveys ● Focus Groups

Qualitative Forecast Methods

Qualitative approaches are frequently used when an organization is entering new markets, or creating new products or services, where no factual, historic data exist. The *Delphi method* is an opinion-based forecast method that anonymously polls a panel of experts for their forecasts. The experts are deliberately kept apart, and they are unknown to each other, because group dynamics and discussion may distort and reduce creativity. These experts are asked a series of questions regarding the topic. Each expert then prepares a written response to each question, along with supporting arguments. Each participant receives anonymous copies of all the other experts' responses. The experts are invited to revise or defend their responses. The revisions are submitted to the researcher, who repeats the process, perhaps as many as three or four times, until a consensus develops.

Sport-Obermeyer, a designer and manufacturer of sports apparel, has used a modified Delphi approach successfully for a number of years. Forecast accuracy is critical to Sport-Obermeyer, because it must commit to production for the following fall's orders by February. It uses independent forecasts from six members of a committee. Rather than seeking consensus in subsequent forecast rounds, Sport-Obermeyer averages the expert opinion. Over time, it has found that when the six forecasts are in general agreement, the average result is very accurate. When the forecasts do not agree, the average is inaccurate.[7]

Other types of qualitative methods include surveying the sales and marketing personnel, obtaining expert opinions, and using intuition. Relying on instinct or "gut feel" is something that many successful managers and top executives frequently do. It has recently become more acceptable to admit using intuition to support key decisions.[8]

Quantitative Forecast Methods

Quantitative forecasting methods use historical, numerical data to predict future events. Several types of quantitative forecast methods are presented in the following:

Causal Modeling – This type of quantitative forecasting uses historical data to identify cause-and-effect relationships among key variables. Causal modeling tries to identify what market conditions and organizational activities affect product or service demand factors. An example of a cause-and-effect relationship is that if the economy is growing, unemployment is likely to be down. Although this relationship may seem obvious, there is probably not a one-to-one rela-tionship. Causal modeling helps to identify the direction and the strength of the relationship between variables so that demand patterns can be reasonably predicted.

Correlation/regression analysis is a type of causal modeling that uses historical patterns to describe the nature and the degree of the relationship between two variables. The correlation coefficient indi-cates whether the relationship is positive (that is, both variables change in the same direction) or negative (that is, one variable increases while the other decreases). With the use of a regression equation, one can predict how a change in one variable (the inde-pendent variable, which in this case is economic growth) affects a change in the other, dependent variable (unemployment). Myriad computer programs, such as Statistical Package for the Social Sciences (SPSS), are available to help identify the patterns.

Time Series Analysis – This quantitative approach models how data behave over time, and it looks for relationships and patterns among the data. Time series analyses for costs, prices, inventories, interest rates, and employment are important to business, because they can be used to extract information regarding patterns that might be time-related. Time series analysis may break down data into sepa-rate elements, and each element may follow its own pattern. The components of a time series include long-term trends, seasonal vari-ations, cyclical variations, and random errors. An understanding of the causes underlying the patterns must be developed in order to accurately forecast using time series data. For instance, is the observed data fluctuation an indication of seasonal variation (for example, snowmobile sales), a longer-term general business or eco-nomic variation, or an indicator of a long-term trend (for example, the result of a sustained decrease in demand)? Or is the fluctuation the result of random sampling or an error?

The answer may include several of these factors. Data may be smoothed and seasonally adjusted to remove these influences, with the objective of developing an understanding of the long-term under-lying trend. Three common smoothing methods are moving average, weighted moving average, and exponential smoothing. A *moving average* approach simply takes the average of the most current "n" periods, so that for each period, the most current data are added and the oldest data are removed. *Weighted moving average* gives differing weights to each observation of actual demand included in the forecast. More weight is generally given to more recent periods to reflect trend data. *Exponential smoothing* is another weighted method that weights the demand for the most recent period and the forecast for the previous period as a basis for the current forecast.

Many organizations use programs that capture demand history and create time series forecasts. Hirshfield's, a regional decorating center with more than 20 retail locations, is one such organization. Hirshfield's uses a computer-modeling program to help determine its demand forecast based on history. The model Hirshfield's uses captures seasonality in demand, and it uses exponential smoothing to help forecast future needs. It makes sense to give recent demand patterns a heavier weight in a trendy industry like decorating, where preferred wallcovering colors and designs change with home fashion trends. The computer model recommends optimal order quantity based on both forecast data and economic order quantity issues.

Market Research Data – As a forecast method, market research can involve introducing a potential new product or service in a test market and gauging consumer response. This method was popular with consumer products companies in the 1980s, but it has decreased because test marketing tips off the competition and delays the new product's introduction. Consumer surveys may also be conducted, either by mail, telephone, or in person. Organizations also interview small groups of consumers in focus groups to obtain an understanding of trends, issues, and interests. The data gathered from market research efforts might be a combination of qualitative and quantitative data.

Factors That Can Affect Forecasts

Any forecast is accurate only as long as conditions remain unchanged. In other words, forecast errors are a way of life. Factors that can affect the accuracy of forecasts include war and threats of war, strikes and threats of strikes, natural factors such as disasters, and discoveries and the depletion of natural resources. Other issues for consideration include changes in technology, government, and law, as well as changes in the population or consumer taste. These and other commodity-specific factors must be considered and tracked for each of an organization's critical raw materials or components.

One of the factors that created significant forecast errors for many industries in the late 1990s was the growth and development of the Internet. The Internet and e-commerce sharply shifted demand away from traditional channels in many sectors, such as personal computers and books. Such major shifts are difficult to predict. Those who predict the trends or can respond to changes quickly come out as the winners. Other technological shifts — for instance, the move away from the dedicated word-processing machines of the 1970s and 1980s to personal computers — took companies such as Wang, the leader in word processing, by surprise. Wang did not survive the transition.

Changes in the economy and business environment create situations such as fluctuation in leadtimes. When leadtimes change, buying organizations are left with either material shortages or the need to carry larger inventories to protect the organization from delivery uncertainty. Both of these increase costs and decrease flexibility, so neither is acceptable in today's globally competitive economy. Economic changes also can affect the availability of qualified labor. This was a problem in the late 1990s, as unemployment reached record lows. More predictable are labor agreement expirations. These are reported in the ISM *Report On Business*® and other sources. Strikes or threats of strikes can result in dramatic market changes. Advance warning of such potential supply constrictions allows a purchasing and supply manager to take protective action. The issues in an organization's internal and external environment that could affect its forecasts are nearly endless.

Implications of Forecasting for Purchasing

Effective purchasing performance is highly dependent on timely and accurate forecast data. Before using any forecast, the purchaser should understand:

- The assumptions underlying the forecast
- The source of the forecast data
- Who is accountable for the accuracy of the forecast
- When the forecast was made

- Whether any significant changes have occurred since the forecast was made
- The historical validity of the forecast versus actual performance

Without understanding the data, costly mistakes can be made.

One approach to reducing the risk of inaccurate forecasts is to require suppliers to hold extra inventory either on-site or at their location. This approach simply pushes the forecast responsibility to the supplier, which is further away from the source of demand and likely to have even less accurate forecast information than the buying organization.

Another way to deal with uncertainty is to change the environment in which an organization does business. National Bicycle, a Japanese manufacturer of high-priced bicycles, began to suffer when it was faced with inexpensive bicycles from its competition. Rather than compete in the mass bicycle market and carry large inventories, National became a custom, make-to-order bicycle manufacturer. Customers have 2 million possible combinations of options to choose from, including custom sizing, to get the perfect bicycle. They receive their bikes within two weeks 99.99 percent of the time.[9] Such innovative options are not available, or of interest, to everyone.

Sharing forecast data with multiple levels of the supply chain is increasingly common today. By using shared data, suppliers can better anticipate demand and meet the buying organization's needs on a more timely and efficient basis. Waste in the supply chain is reduced, and everyone, especially the final customer, benefits. Wal-Mart has been a leader in sharing data with its suppliers. Suppliers use actual demand data to determine how much to ship to Wal-Mart, rather than Wal-Mart placing an order. This has resulted in improved inventory turns and performance.

Another approach to reducing the need for accurate short-term forecasts is to employ a "pull" production system, as presented in Chapter 3. Items are not ordered until they are needed; they are pulled through the system by customer demand. This approach only works well in environments of relatively stable demand or short leadtimes. For purchasers, the need for accurate forecast data increases in direct proportion to the length of the leadtime for the items needed.

As data management continues to improve and more organizations see the benefit of sharing forecasts with suppliers, forecast accuracy will improve. However, in today's rapidly changing business environment, characterized by continual change and shorter product and service life cycles, the need for accuracy has also accelerated. Forecasting will continue to be a challenge for purchasing, and organizations as a whole, for years to come.

Key Points

1. Forecasting is an important method for predicting and managing the effect of future events.
2. The key issues that affect the type of forecast needed are the reason for the forecast, the nature of the item or the trend being forecast, and the time horizon of the forecast.
3. Economic issues play a key role in the development of forecasts. Due to increased globalization, organizations throughout the world must be concerned about their own country's economy as well as the global economy.
4. Economic indicators provide insight into key business trends. Many of these economic indicators are available from the U.S. government on its Web sites.
5. The use of indices is a common way to show economic changes and trends. The most frequently used economic indices in the United States are the Consumer Price Index (CPI), the Producer Price Index (PPI), and the Implicit Price Deflator, also known as the GNP deflator.
6. The ISM *Report On Business*® (Manufacturing and Non-Manufacturing) is one of the most widely used and respected economic indicators. It is published monthly by the Institute for Supply Management™, based on input from hundreds of purchasers throughout the United States.
7. The U.S. government provides a wealth of data on economic trends and history that is useful for developing forecasts. Most of

the data is available online through the Bureau of Labor Statistics (www.bls.gov) and its linkages to other government Web sites.

8. Forecasts developed by organizations include both macro (broad and long-range projections) and micro (specific and near-term projections) issues.
9. Organizations may use qualitative forecast techniques, quantitative forecast techniques, or a combination of both, depending on the availability and relevance of historic data.
10. Myriad factors affect the accuracy of forecasts. While these rapidly changing times make forecasting more difficult, they also make forecasting more important.
11. Purchasers can help their organizations reduce the risk of forecast errors in a number of ways, including building buffer stocks and improving information sharing with suppliers and customers.

Questions for Review

1. What are the major areas of concern for purchasing and supply management in forecasting?
2. Describe the differences among leading, lagging, and coincident economic indicators, and provide examples of each.
3. Describe three global economic issues that can have an impact on the accuracy of forecasts.
4. Describe the difference between the Consumer Price Index and the Producer Price Index. Which is more appropriate to use in business forecasts, and why?
5. Describe qualitative and quantitative forecasting, and explain when each method is appropriate.

For Additional Information

Diebold, F.X. *Elements of Forecasting*, South-Western Publications, New Mexico, 1997.

Hanke, J.E. *Business Forecasting*, Prentice Hall, New York, NY, 1998.

Madrikas, S.G. Ed. and S.C. Wheelright. *Forecasting Methods and Applications*, John Wiley and Sons, New York, NY, 1998.

Vollman, T.E., W.L. Berry, and C. Whybark. *Integrated Production and Inventory Management*, Business One Irwin, Homewood, IL, 1993, Chapter 3, "Short-Term Forecasting Systems."

Endnotes

1. Porter, M. *Competitive Advantage*, Harvard Business School Press, Boston, MA, 1979.
2. Zsidisin, G. and L.M. Ellram. "Supply Risk Assessment Analysis," *Practix: Best Practices in Purchasing and Supply Chain Management*, June 1999, pp. 9-12.
3. Fine, C. Clockspeed, Perseus Books, Reading, MA, 1998.
4. Porter, M. *The Competitive Advantage of Nations*, Harvard Business School Press, Boston, MA, 1986.
5. Kauffman, R. "Indicator Qualities of the NAPM Report On Business®," *The Journal of Supply Chain Management*, (35: 2), Spring 1999, pp. 29-37.
6. Fisher, M.L. "What is the Right Supply Chain for Your Product?" *Harvard Business Review*, March-April 1997, pp. 105-116.
7. Fisher, 1997.
8. Shapiro, S. and M.T. Spence. "Managerial Intuition: A Conceptual and Operational Framework," *Business Horizons*, January-February 1997, pp. 64-68.
9. Shapiro and Spence, 1997, pp. 115-116.

CHAPTER 8

PURCHASING INFORMATION AND STRATEGY DEVELOPMENT

How does purchasing plan, develop, and maintain strategies?

Chapter Objectives

- To understand the importance of maintaining an awareness of the external market
- To be aware of the various buying strategies that purchasers pursue and the strategies' relative merits
- To become familiar with a number of techniques for implementing purchasing strategies
- To understand the importance of forecasts in planning and implementing strategies
- To be aware of revenue-generating opportunities
- To understand the importance of supply chain management and to take a holistic approach to purchasing strategy

Introduction

As emphasized throughout this volume, the role of purchasing and supply management (PSM) has been elevated in many organizations. With the recognition of the role of purchasing as a value-enhancing function, the elevation of purchasing will continue to increase in the future. This final chapter addresses the importance of maintaining market awareness while planning, developing, and implementing strategy. The latter part of the chapter addresses leading-edge concepts, such as purchasing as a revenue-generating function, and discusses how supply chain management is shaping the way that organizations compete.

Market Awareness

An important role of purchasing as a boundary-spanning function is to develop and maintain an awareness of market trends, technology trends, and other external factors that shape the way organizations buy.

Rationale for Market Awareness

The need for purchasers to be aware of market issues and trends seems obvious in today's rapidly changing competitive environment. Many of the concepts presented in this section were discussed in depth in Chapter 5, as part of early supplier involvement. The following are important reasons for purchasers to stay in touch with the market:

Understanding Market Capacity and Supply Forecasts – Many markets shift rapidly due to economic and environmental changes, and the purchaser must be in touch with the market to ensure that his or her organization's forecasted needs can be met. For example, if a shortage is anticipated, the purchaser may want to establish a long-term supply contract to gain supply assurance.

In some cases, the events can be anticipated, as available market capacity gradually shrinks or declines based on gradual economic changes. Being aware of market trends alerts the purchaser to potential supplier problems, such as impending labor disputes, supplier liquidity problems, and suppliers that are entering and exiting the market. Some events may be unanticipated, such as the 1999 earthquake in Taiwan that sent the price of some computer parts and components skyrocketing.

Developing Alternate Sources – Because all market shifts cannot be anticipated, developing alternate sources or alternate locations for suppliers is important. Backup sources allow the purchaser greater supply assurance; they reduce the risk of putting "all your eggs in one basket." By researching and staying in touch with the market, purchasers can identify the best available alternative sources.

Developing Supplier Profiles – For current and potential suppliers, profiles can identify each supplier's capabilities, capacities, and relative strengths. The profiles can help to identify alternate sources, as well as to alert researchers and designers of new developments in the marketplace. At Hewlett-Packard's Vancouver Division, which manufactures printers, the engineers welcome purchasing's insights into new suppliers, new technologies, and new ideas. Because the engineers have become busier due to increasingly rapid product changes, their reliance on purchasing has increased.[1]

Providing Technological Updates – Technological updates from current suppliers, as well as from suppliers that are not currently part of the organization's supply base, are another important contribution that purchasing can make to enhance its value to the organization.

Supporting New Product and Service Development – All of the preceding factors are useful in refining the organization's current products, services, and processes. However, technology updates, readily available supplier profiles, and an understanding of market capacity and supply needs are essential in supporting the development of new products and services. Purchasing must be aware of market trends, issues, and potential as new products are being designed and developed, to ensure that the best available technology and processes are integrated into the new product or service, as presented in Chapter 6. Purchasing must be aware of the major risks that could impede the successful rollout of new products and services, such as supplier quality or reliability problems. Purchasing must also monitor supplier progress in relation to market trends throughout the product life cycle.

The new product or service development process is so critical that some organizations, such as Honda of America Manufacturing and Intel, have assigned dedicated supply personnel throughout the new product design, development, and rollout process. After the product or service has been introduced, responsibility for the new product or service is handed off to another purchasing group that continues to monitor and manage risk.[2]

Techniques for Monitoring Trends and Managing the Data

The amount of available market information is growing exponentially. Chapter 7 presented the myriad of resources for external information related to economic trends and economic data. Some of these sources, such as the ISM *Report On Business*®, provide data on market expansion or contraction as well as general price trends.

Trade periodicals are an excellent source of industry-specific information on trends, new technologies, sources, and even targeted advertising. These publications are specific to an industry, and they include such titles as *Electronic Buyer's News*, *Computerworld*, and *Packaging News*, to name a few.

Trade periodicals may be published by trade associations or independent organizations. Regardless, trade associations are also an excellent source of information. *The Encyclopedia of Associations* lists all of the major industry associations in the United States. It might be worthwhile for purchasers to join one or more industry associations for the items associated with significant areas of organizational spending.

Trade shows, also known as merchandise shows, can also be an excellent source of information on new suppliers, new technologies, and trends. These shows vary in focus. With the goal of promoting business in a certain region, trade shows can encompass a variety of industries. Others are directed at developing minority businesses or specific industries. It is important to understand the nature and goals of the trade show, and how it meets purchasing's goals.

The Internet is another source of information on industries and technologies. The key to the Internet is finding the data. In many cases, that involves knowing what keywords to use in searches. Industry Web sites can provide links to related company Web sites, and vice versa. Company Web sites allow purchasers to identify an organization's key products, services, and capabilities, thus saving time in screening suppliers and identifying key opportunities. Both ISM's Web site (www.ism.ws) and *Purchasing* magazine's Web site (www.purchasing.com) provide excellent links to industry Web sites and articles. Many companies also have extranets for their suppliers to access information about the organization's plans, forecast data, and so on. Some organizations, such as Deere and Company, have secure Web sites that allow suppliers to access data specific to them.

Professional associations and professional networking can also provide excellent data. By networking with other purchasing and supply management professionals in noncompeting organizations, buyers can identify hot new technologies and trends.

As purchasing gathers important and useful market data, it is important to identify how the information can be used by the organization. Thus, the buyers need to identify who might find the data beneficial, as well as how to get the information into the right hands.

Dissemination of Information Throughout the Organization

Data can only become information if it is transformed in a way that makes it meaningful and useful to the organization. Thus, purchasing must develop a plan for getting the right data to the right people.

Company Intranet Web Pages – These pages can be an excellent means for purchasing to disseminate data in large organizations. Such sites may include information on policies, best practices, training, and even procedures manuals. Companies such as American Express and Baxter Health Care Corporation have developed extensive intranets in order to communicate information to their PSM professionals throughout the world. It is often difficult to cut through the "clutter" of such Web sites to focus on what is meaningful, so Web sites should be organized clearly. It is a good idea to send users an e-mail notifying them when significant updates have been made.

Company Newsletters – Although widely disseminated, company newsletters may suffer from the same problems as Web sites. Purchasing may want to develop a newsletter or Web site dedicated to technology and market issues that is organized clearly and specifically into technology, product, or service groups. The purchasing organizations at Deere and Company, General Motors, and DaimlerChrysler all produce newsletters directed specifically at supply issues. The newsletters are disseminated to company employees as well as suppliers throughout the world.

Networking and Team Meetings – One-on-one contact with other functional areas is often the best way to disseminate data. Many organizations, such as DaimlerChrysler, are organized in cross-disciplinary teams so that regular communication occurs among purchasing and the other disciplines that would be concerned with the data gathered by purchasing.

If no formalized mechanisms for communication are in place, purchasing should contact the marketing, engineering, design, or other personnel who might be interested in purchasing's data. By showing personal interest in supporting other functions, purchasing demonstrates its value enhancement capability. Thus, purchasing and supply management is more likely to be involved and, as a result, asked for information in the future. This information also helps with setting strategy.

Buying Strategies

Among the strategies available to purchasing and supply managers is purchase timing. The use of market forecast data can assist in the selection of the appropriate option from those listed in the following.

Hand-to-Mouth Buying

This short-term strategy is typically described as the purchase of requirements for immediate needs — just enough to cover the lead-time between the time of order and the time the item is needed. This strategy might be employed in falling markets where buyers want to take advantage of decreasing prices with each successive purchase. As presented in Chapter 2, cash flow constraints may also mandate *hand-to-mouth* buying, particularly if the organization has a long cash-to-cash cycle or if a government organization is at the end of a budget period or its spending limits. This strategy may also be desirable for perishable goods and goods that have uncertain future demand. Finally, goods that are subject to rapid technological change or "fashion" items that may experience sharp price declines are also suited to hand-to-mouth buying.

Buying to Current Requirements

Advance purchases for use in the three-week to three-month timeframe might be classified as *buying to current requirements*. In these circumstances, the amount purchased covers the organization's production or sales forecast. This practice is fairly common. It ensures current supply while avoiding excessive inventory carrying costs. The downside is that if the market changes and purchased items become scarce, it might be difficult for the organization to secure them, because no long-term commitments have been made. This is one reason, as presented in the previous sections, that it is critical for buyers to stay abreast of both current forecasts and market conditions and trends.

Forward Buying

Conditions such as potential supply constrictions or inflationary markets may develop. The purchaser might become aware of such potential pressures by monitoring the market using the approaches presented in Chapter 7 and earlier in this chapter. This may cause purchasing managers to hedge prices or supply by buying more of a product than is needed to meet current requirements. This practice is called *forward buying*, and it protects the organization from shortages or delays the impact of rising prices. The trade-offs are, of course, increased inventory carrying costs, potential obsolescence, and the risk that the market may shift in the opposite direction. The proactive purchasing manager will evaluate the trade-off between inventory carrying cost increases or other cost factors and the decreased risk of supply constriction or decreased prices when using this strategy. This strategy is frequently pursued in purchases of chemicals and plastics/polymers when the market is tightening. The intent of this strategy is to use the purchased item internally.

Speculative Buying

Speculative buying refers to purchases made with the intent to resell them at a later date for a profit. These speculative goods may be the same as those purchased for consumption, but the quantities purchased will be in excess of current or future needs. Speculative buying takes advantage of expected price increases to profit from the resale of the goods. This approach is common in commodity markets, such as coffee and grain, where there is easy access to the market and the contracts are purchased. Here, the speculative buyer may not even take possession before reselling the item. Many organizations specifically forbid speculative purchasing. In general, speculative buying should not be undertaken without management approval.

Volume Purchase Agreements

When significant, known quantities of specific products or commodities are needed, these requirements may be met through volume purchase agreements. The primary objectives of these agreements are to ensure supply and to consolidate requirements to maximize purchase leverage. Depending on the duration of the demand, these agreements may be either short- or long-term. Differing by circumstance, these agreements range from specific descriptions of the volumes to be purchased to "very nebulous descriptions." In some industries, such as canned vegetables, volume purchase agreements may be developed 12 to 18 months before the item is needed, because the grower needs to prepare the soil, obtain the seeds, plant, and harvest. If an organization decides it needs significant quantities of lima beans in three months, it will likely pay a tremendous premium.

Life-of-Product or Life-of-Part Supply

For numerous reasons, it may be desirable to develop and award contracts to suppliers of raw materials or components for the expected life of the item produced. For example, if duration of need is limited, it may not be cost-effective to rebid. Other reasons for this type of contract are familiarity with the requirements and the use of the purchased item and special supplier capabilities. In some cases, a significant investment in capital, tooling, and the training of personnel is required in order to produce specialized items or services. It would be costly to duplicate this investment multiple times, and there could be significant supplier inefficiencies during the learning period. Life-of-product/part agreements are often developed between buyers and suppliers with a long, collaborative history, which may include such activities as concurrent engineering of the components, supplier colocation, and early supplier involvement. These agreements are common in the automotive industry and the heavy/farm equipment industry, including companies such as John Deere or Caterpillar.

In some cases, such as software development, life of "program" agreements are inevitable due to the extremely high cost to switch suppliers. Buyers should consider the difficulty of switching when developing long-term agreements.

Just-In-Time

Just-In-Time (JIT) manufacturing is more a philosophy of doing business than a specific technique. The JIT philosophy focuses on identifying and eliminating waste wherever it is found in the manufacturing system. The concept of continuous improvement becomes the central managerial focus. One of the more highly publicized results of JIT implementation is the initiation of a "pull" system of manufacturing, where items are manufactured to meet demand or specific customer orders rather than "pushed" into inventory. This results in significant reductions of raw material, work-in-progress, and finished goods inventories; significant reductions in throughput time; and large decreases in the amount of space required for the manufacturing process.

The greatest improvement for an organization implementing JIT, however, is usually related to quality. If there is little or no raw material inventory, incoming raw material and components must be of impeccable quality or manufacturing will grind to a halt. Similarly, due to a lack of work-in-process inventory, each intermediate manufacturing step must yield high-quality output, or the process will stop.

JIT philosophy focuses on the elimination of waste wherever it is found in the business system, including the supplier. The aim is to reduce waste and cost throughout the entire supply chain. If a manufacturer decides that it will no longer carry raw material inventory, and that henceforth its suppliers must carry the inventory, this does not reduce supply chain cost. It merely transfers costs from one link in the supply chain to another. While those additional inventory carrying costs may be borne, short-term, by the supplier, they eventually must be passed on to the buying organization, and ultimately the customer, in the form of higher prices.

One commonly cited reason for difficulties in the implementation of JIT is a lack of cooperation from suppliers, due to the changes required of each supplier's system. Suppliers need to change from traditional quality control inspection practices to the implementation of statistical process control. Also, suppliers are asked to manufacture in other than their usual lot sizes and to make frequent deliveries of small lots with precise timing. Further, the supplier may be required to provide the buyer access to a great deal of information that traditionally had been considered confidential. This may include access to its master production schedule, shop floor schedule, material requirements planning system, managerial system, and, in some cases, even its financial statements. Clearly, purchasers must be cooperative and persuasive in converting supply chains to JIT operations.

Supplier selection, single sourcing, supplier management, and supplier communication are critical issues for purchasers and supply managers in implementing JIT. Key issues in supplier selection for JIT include supplier quality control methods, proximity of manufacturing facilities, manufacturing flexibility, and reliability. Due to its intense nature, JIT firms and their suppliers tend to develop collaborative relationships supported by long-term, single-source contracts. The concept of partnering is often applied to the JIT buyer-supplier relationship.

Following supplier selection, careful supplier performance measurement and management often lead to supplier certification, a designation reserved for suppliers that have proved their quality, on-time delivery, and reliability over long periods of time. Supplier certification can eliminate the need for all incoming inspections, further supporting the JIT process.

Close, frequent buyer-supplier communication is essential in effective JIT operations. Suppliers are given long-range insight into the buyer's production schedule. The schedule may span a dozen weeks or more, with the nearest several weeks' schedule frozen. This allows the supplier to acquire raw materials in a stockless production mode and to supply the buyer without inventory buildups. Suppliers provide daily updates of progress and production schedules and problems.

The function of the purchasing department is significantly changed under a JIT philosophy — from the processing of orders to supplier selection and long-term contract negotiation. Many times, the close communication needed for JIT is supported with electronic data interchange (EDI) capabilities or secure extranets, where companies share information about requirements and suppliers have direct access to forecast data.

Consignment

Inventories that are owned by a supplier but are stored at the buyer's facility are considered consignment inventories. These goods are billed to the buyer only after they have been consumed. This practice became popular in the late 1990s. The buyer does not have to show consignment inventory on its books (specifically, the balance sheet). The buyer also does not tie up its working capital in inventory until the consignment inventory is actually work-in-process or otherwise consumed.

At first glance, this practice seems to be advantageous to both buyer and supplier. The supplier has an assured sale, while the buyer has the security of on-site inventory without inventory investment. There are, however, potential problems with this procedure. For example, even though consignment inventory is stored at the buyer's warehouse, it is still owned by the supplier. As such, the supplier may want to remove some items to sell to another customer. Meanwhile the buyer, whose facility stores the goods, is counting on those items to cover his or her own requirements. Phelps Dodge, a major copper mining company, developed a win-win solution for consignment inventories with its largest tire supplier, Michelin. Phelps Dodge has given Michelin secure space to store its tires. Michelin is allowed to store tires for Phelps Dodge as well as for other customers, saving Michelin the cost of renting storage space while Phelps Dodge enjoys the benefits of on-site, consigned inventory.

The fact that the buyer does not invest in consignment inventory, but only pays as items are used, does not relieve the buying organization of inventory carrying costs. The purchasing organization needs to provide a secure facility for consignment inventory, care for it, and perhaps track it. In addition, the supplier will most assuredly "adjust" the price it charges for items to reflect the fact that its working capital is tied up in "idle" inventory for a longer period. The organization must also consider the financial stability and cost of capital of the supplier. If a supplier has cash flow problems or a high cost of capital, requiring consigned inventory could "push" the supplier over the edge into financial instability.

Commodities

In the purest sense, commodities are homogeneous items that can easily be graded or classified. They have often had limited processing (except in the case of metals, which are processed from ore to generic metal) and are generally treated as raw materials. Commodities include items such as copper, gold, silver, coffee, grain, and so on. These non-branded, generic items are easily interchangeable within each class.

Distinguishing features of commodities are that, in most cases, the market for commodities closely resembles that of pure competition. There are many buyers and suppliers. In general, no one buyer or supplier is so powerful that it can influence the market, and information is readily available concerning market prices and supply levels. There are notable exceptions. For example, the Hunt brothers unsuccessfully tried to corner the silver market in the late 1970s. The Organization of Petroleum Exporting Countries (OPEC) influences the market as a group, not as individual countries. These examples do not fit the requirements for pure competition, because a buyer (Hunt brothers) or a supplier (OPEC) yields market power.

Commodity exchanges, such as the grain exchanges in Minneapolis and Chicago, are the venue for buying and selling commodities. As with the New York Stock Exchange, only a certain number of "seats" are available, and highly qualified and aggressive buyers compete to get the best prices for the items they need.

Like the foreign exchange market, commodity exchanges allow a buyer to purchase the item today (spot market), in the future (forward market), or to buy options to purchase or sell an item at a certain price in the future. With options, there is no commitment to buy — purchasers buy the right to choose to buy at a certain price at a set future date. If the market price is higher than the "call" price of the option, it makes sense for the purchaser to buy at the call price. Purchasers could even make money by reselling. If the market price goes down below the "call" price, purchasers are under no obligation to buy. They just let the option expire. The only thing that they have lost is the money they paid for the option initially, which could be substantial.

Supplier Replenishment Systems

Supplier replenishment systems are known by many names: supplier-managed inventory, vendor-managed inventory, supplier stocking programs, and the like. The key is that the supplier manages the inventory ordering and replenishment in the purchasing organization's facility. There are several advantages to such an approach:

1. The supplier gains expertise in an organization's inventory usage patterns, increasing in-stock availability.
2. It eliminates duplication of ordering efforts by the organization and the supplier, saving effort, time, and money.
3. Because the supplier understands the usage of its item, it is able to suggest alternatives and improvements.
4. It frees purchasing time to focus on more value-adding issues.
5. It substantially reduces paperwork through consolidated billing and the elimination of paper orders.

This approach is most common among distributors or multiline suppliers that carry a wide number of items that the organization purchases. It would not otherwise be worth the buyer's or supplier's time and effort. Supplier replenishment programs are common for packaging raw materials, components, and supplies of all types.

In some cases, the distributor may take over the responsibility of many distributors and suppliers, providing a single source for all of the organization's maintenance, repair, and operating (MRO) supplies. This is frequently referred to as "integrated supply."

Outsourcing

As discussed in Chapter 1, outsourcing is an important strategic decision as well as an important buying strategy. Outsourcing has become increasingly common as companies focus their efforts on their core competencies, leaving other activities to external organizations. Outsourcing is an approach that should be undertaken with great care, because it can be costly and difficult to reverse.

Implementation Techniques

Several common techniques for the implementation of purchasing strategies are based on forecast data.

Hedging

The concept of hedging was briefly introduced in the section on commodity markets. Hedging typically involves the sale of a futures contract to offset the purchase of a cash commodity. It can also involve the purchase of a futures contract to offset the sale of a cash commodity, which is part of an end product sold by the organization. An organization simultaneously enters into two contracts of an opposite nature: one in a cash market for the sale or purchase of an item, and one in a futures market to "protect" the price of the item being sold or purchased.

Hedging is used to safeguard profit margins, for example, when a sales contract with fixed prices and extended delivery is negotiated, but the purchase of the raw material used in the manufacture of that item is postponed. If material prices were to rise between the time of the order and the purchase of the raw material used in production, the profitability of the contract could be jeopardized. Hedging is also used to protect inventory values when the price of raw materials is declining. If declining raw materials prices cause finished product prices to fall, the organization will lose money due to its relatively higher cost of raw materials. With a futures contract, the organization can insure itself against price fluctuations in commodity-like raw materials.

For example, assume that a company contracts in January for the construction of a building to be completed by November. The building includes 50,000 pounds of copper pipes, which were included in the bid price at $1.04 per pound. Because of the construction lead-time, the copper will not be needed until August. To guard against a possible increase in the price of copper, the purchasing manager buys an August futures contract for 50,000 pounds of copper at $1.10 per pound, which is the January price of copper for delivery in August. If the spot (cash) price rises, typically the futures price will rise by a similar amount. If, in this example, the spot price rises 6 cents per pound by August, and the August futures price will also rise 6 cents per pound, the futures contract can be sold for a 6 cents per pound profit, which offsets the rise of 6 cents in the price of spot copper when the purchasing manager buys the copper in August.

Spot Buying

Spot buying is the practice of buying a commodity on the "spot" or open market. This means buying the commodity for delivery in the near future, generally 30 days or less. This approach is common when a company experiences unexpected demand or prefers not to commit to a future purchase due to uncertainty in its future requirements or anticipated price decreases.

Dollar Averaging

When purchasing a commodity or component over time, the value of the items in inventory may be treated as an average, based on the mix of quantities and the prices of items bought at different times. Whether prices are averaged, treated as first-in, first-out, or treated as last-in, first-out depends on the inventory valuation rules the organization follows. Using the averaging approach, if 20,000 pounds of copper are bought at $1.04 per pound, 14,000 pounds are bought at $1.07 per pound, and 26,000 pounds are bought at $1.09 per pound, the average price of the commodity would be $1.069 per pound. Averaging the price of copper dampens the effect of short-term price fluctuations, smoothing the overall average price.

Contractual Agreements

The supplier selection and ordering process can be costly and time-consuming unless some routines are established, as presented in the first volume in this series. Rather than selecting a supplier and placing an order each time a requirement occurs, many organizations use longer-term agreements for ongoing purchases. Such contractual agreements typically involve products or services with ongoing consumption. Contracts may also be written to cover families of products or services or classifications of products or services, such as office supplies, cleaning and janitorial supplies, electrical supplies, or temporary labor. Agreements such as this may take many different forms, including multiyear contracts, life-of-product contracts, future delivery agreements, and contracts for a percentage of a supplier's capacity, or even options on products or capacities.

Long-Term Contracting

If using world-class suppliers is required to provide an organization a competitive advantage, the long-term relationships that are formed with those suppliers will typically be preserved with long-term contracts or agreements. Several types of these agreements and their options are discussed in the following:

Price-Change Clauses – These clauses are designed to protect the buyer and the supplier from market price changes during the contract term. In any long-term contract, both parties are at risk from input cost changes. A buying organization would not want to agree to a fixed-price contract only to watch the worldwide price of the basic raw material input fall significantly. The supplier, likewise, would be harmed by entering into a long-term agreement only to find labor or raw materials prices rising. The mechanism for sharing such risks is called a *price-change clause* (or an escalation or de-escalation clause), which provides for price adjustments based on indices that reflect material and labor cost changes. This clause is an important element in a long-term contract. Without such a clause, the agreement may quickly become unattractive to one or both parties. It is an equitable method of ensuring mutual risk sharing of economic changes that are beyond the parties' control. Many price-change clauses do not share risk or cost change burdens equally. This imbalance in risk sharing can lead to the demise of a contract, and it puts pressure on the buyer-supplier relationship.

Life-of-Product or Service Contracts – One of the options for long-term contracting is to agree with suppliers to provide materials, components, or services not for a specific time period, but for the entire life span of the product or service.

Life-of-product contracts can be useful in developing cooperation between a buyer and a supplier for products that have short life cycles, that are highly complex, or for which technology is rapidly changing. For longer-term situations, this type of contract allows the supplier to recover its investment in necessary equipment and technology over a reasonable time period.

Multiyear Contracting – More frequently, buyer and supplier organizations are entering into close, collaborative relationships based on mutual benefits. Buyers are reducing their supply bases to include only the suppliers that are judged to be superior. In such cases, it is likely that the organizations will enter into agreements that include options to renew their contracts once the original contract expires. The initial contract and each extension may span several years. For example, Kodak entered into an agreement in which IBM manages its information technology and associated infrastructure. The original agreement, which commenced in the early 1990s, was extended multiple times, finally through the year 2000.[3] Some purchasing managers may enter into contracts of a six- to 10-year duration. These contracts often include long-term commitments in the information technology arena. An example of this includes a contract that American Express recently negotiated with one of its key mainframe software suppliers. The key factor in multiyear contracting is the selection of such long-term partners/suppliers; the selection process often takes six to 12 months. This time and effort should be viewed as a long-term investment, because the selection process need not be repeated until the multiyear contract nears expiration.

It is important for purchasing and supply managers to be sure that, in the formulation of such long-term agreements, provisions are made for specific, periodic performance and satisfaction reviews by both parties. In the case of the IBM-Kodak agreement, which involves hundreds of IBM employees managing Kodak's information technology on-site, a multiple-level communication and management process was set up. The process includes weekly, monthly, and quarterly reviews by progressively higher levels of management, along with a formal annual assessment.[4] It allowed for the early identification and resolution of potential problems or discrepancies. Problems must be addressed in a timely and orderly fashion. As with any long-term agreement, provisions for dissolution should be agreed upon prior to the contract signing.

Future Delivery Contracting

A purchasing manager's organization may have sporadic requirements that, nevertheless, are of major importance. In such cases, a buyer may want to ensure that the goods will be available from a particular supplier. A future delivery contract can be negotiated to ensure that productive capacity is reserved. Sole-source suppliers of such items as capital equipment may fall into this category. Price-change clauses, as discussed previously, are critical to these contracts.

As mentioned in the first part of this chapter, agriculture items frequently are purchased using future contracts. This is critical due to the long leadtime required to plant, grow, and harvest.

Use of Options

A purchase option is the right to purchase something under the agreed terms for a specified period of time. When the specified time expires, so does the right to the purchase. Such rights are granted for a negotiable fee, which is forfeited if the right expires without having been exercised.

If an organization is considering a project that has not been finalized, but for which an element has a time or availability constraint, the organization may elect to acquire an option on the critical element. For example, if the construction of a new factory is being considered, a suitable piece of land might be optioned. In exchange for a fee, the interested organization might be given an option to purchase that property until a specified date in the future. Within that time, the buying organization may exercise its option to purchase the property at an agreed price. If the organization decides not to proceed with the project, it is not obliged to purchase the land, but it will forfeit the option fee. Similar types of options are available for some common commodities, such as metals, grains, coffee, and cocoa. These may be purchased on exchanges, as presented earlier in this chapter.

Buying Capacity Reserves

In a rapidly changing business environment, it may not be possible to precisely forecast the specific numbers of products, components, or services that a supplier will be required to provide. In cases where the volume can be estimated, but the exact product mix is unknown, organizations may reserve portions of suppliers' manufacturing capacity or labor pool. This practice ensures the availability of outside, subcontracted manufacturing capacity, even though the precise mix of products to be produced or level of service to be provided will not be known until a later date. This reduces the uncertainty and risk associated with insufficient capacity and the potential for lost sales or poor service levels. The trade-off is the possibility that the full reserved capacity, for which the organization must pay, may not be needed.

Integrated Suppliers

In integrated supply, suppliers come on-site and take over the inventory, including the space required for the inventory and management control of the goods. This relieves the buying organization of having to invest in the inventory until the moment of need. In the railroad industry, this concept has gone to the point where locomotive manufacturers provide and maintain their locomotives, while the railroad pays for "power by the hour." Similarly, Volkswagen has an advanced approach in its Brazilian operations; its suppliers participate in the assembly of automobiles and are paid based on output.

Decision Tree Analysis

A decision tree analysis provides a framework for assessing the subjective probabilities of outcomes and events related to a particular project or purchase. In its simplest form, a decision tree is a diagram that shows several decisions or courses of action and the possible consequences of each. The consequences are called events. In a more elaborate form, the probabilities and the revenues or costs of each event's outcome are estimated, and they are combined to produce an expected value for the event.

The decision tree shown in Figure 8.1 demonstrates how this technique works. In this example, a company is considering whether to develop and market a new product. Development costs are estimated to be $200,000. There is a 0.5 probability that the development effort will succeed and that the product will be marketed. It is also estimated that:

1. If the product is highly successful, it will produce differential income of ($1.5 million minus $300,000 marketing costs) $1.2 million (or a net income of $1 million after subtracting the development cost).

2. If the product is moderately successful, it does a bit better than break even; the income of $500,000 will offset the development and marketing cost by $100,000.

3. If the product is a failure, it will lose $200,000 (or a total loss of $600,000 after taking into account the development and marketing cost).

The estimated probability of high success is 0.4; of moderate success, 0.4; and of failure, 0.2.

FIGURE 8.1
Decision Tree for a New Product Development Process

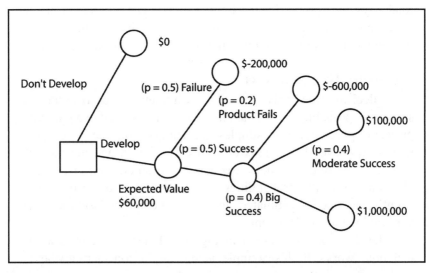

The expected value of each outcome is the monetary income or loss multiplied by the probability of that outcome's occurrence. Thus, the following values are calculated for the example:

1. If development fails, the expected value is the development cost multiplied by the probability of failure: -$200,000 x 0.5 = -$100,000 (that is, a $100,000 loss).

2. If development succeeds, but the product is a failure, the loss is $200,000 in development costs, plus $300,000 in marketing costs, plus $100,000 in obsolete inventory for a total loss of $600,000. The total probability of development success and

product failure is 0.5 x 0.2 = 0.10. The expected value of this outcome is 0.10 x -$600,000 = -$60,000.
3. If development succeeds and the product is moderately successful, the probability is 0.20 (0.5 x 0.4) and the differential net income is $100,000; hence, the expected value is 0.20 x $100,000 = $20,000.
4. If development succeeds and the product is highly successful, the net income is $1 million and the probability is again 0.20; hence, the expected value of this outcome is 0.20 x $1,000,000 = $200,000.

The total expected value of the act of "develop product" is the sum of the expected values of all possible outcomes on the "develop product" branch of the tree ($60,000 + $20,000 + $200,000 = $160,000). This amount is then compared with the expected value of the other alternative act, "don't develop." If the development is not undertaken, there is a 100 percent chance (1.0 probability) that the incremental income will be $0; hence, the expected value of "don't develop" is zero. Because the act "develop product" has the larger expected value, the decision would be to proceed with the development effort. This does not mean, of course, that the ultimate outcome is guaranteed to be a differential income of $160,000. Rather, it means that based on the estimates made in considering this decision, management should assume the risk and go ahead with the development, because the expected payoff is positive. Whereas, if the risk is not taken, there will be zero payoff.

This approach to decisionmaking is powerful if the probabilities can be estimated with reasonable accuracy (or even within a reasonable range). As stated previously, there are virtually no situations where such estimates can be made with sufficient reliability that the decision maker can entirely trust them.

Forecasts of Volume

Based on projected needs, several contract types, supply agreements, and buying strategies may be appropriate. These hand-to-mouth purchases, systems contracts, multiyear supply contracts, life-of-product agreements, and other purchase agreements are tools that buyers use to correlate forecasts of need with supply market conditions.

Determining Annual Requirements

Sales and marketing studies and forecasts, coupled with historical usage data, allow purchasing managers to forecast needs, including raw materials and components, MRO supplies, and capital equipment purchases. Forecasting was presented in Chapter 7.

Part or Product Life

At times, it is useful to forecast volume requirements not by the month or year, but over the entire life of the end product. This part or product life projection can form the basis of life-of-product contracts, and such contracts provide the maximum benefit in terms of volume leverage for the organization.

Supply Markets Relative to Short- and Long-Term Buying Needs

The supply market is constantly changing based on supply and demand, technological changes, changes in consumer preference, and global economic conditions. Purchasers should allow for flexibility in their forecasts and contracts to accommodate these changes.

Supply Chain Management Strategies

Supply chain management is a holistic perspective that considers the flow of information, inventory, and other resources from the earliest recognition of need to the final disposition of an item. This approach to business-to-business relationships and customer service emerged from the field of logistics during the late 1980s and early 1990s. Today, as organizations realize the pivotal role their supply chain trading partners play in their success, the philosophy of supply chain management is taking hold. One focus of supply chain management is to improve demand visibility throughout the supply chain. Improved demand visibility allows all parties in the supply chain — including suppliers, production, logistics, and others — to proactively respond to changes on a real-time basis.

According to Charles Fine,[5] supply chain design is the ultimate source of competitive advantage today. Indeed, the supply chain management concept has been critical in elevating the status of the purchasing function within organizations. This is because of the increased recognition of the importance of purchasing and its critical role in supplier selection and ongoing supplier participation in the design of products, services, processes, and even the supply chain. Companies are now competing supply chain to supply chain.

Supply chain management requires an excellent information flow, such as that made possible by electronic data interchange, enterprise resource planning systems, and the Internet. Thus, supply chain management would have been difficult, if not impossible, before the information technology revolution of the 1990s.

It is likely that supply chain management will continue to grow and evolve as organizations realize the benefits it provides in improved customer service, improved responsiveness, reduced inventory, reduced cycle time, and a host of other areas. In some organizations, such as Arizona Public Service (an electric utility) and Intel, purchasing plays a leading role in shaping supply chain strategy. A key element of supply chain design and strategy development relates to what the company should do internally (make) versus what it should outsource (buy). Make or buy decisions were presented in depth in Chapter 1. Purchasing is in an excellent position to participate in and contribute to the make or buy decision, by identifying potential suppliers along with their strengths and weaknesses. It is also critical, as part of supply chain design, to determine what type of relationship to have with each supplier — from arm's-length to close alliance. Purchasing is also the group best suited to work on supplier relationship management and development.[6]

Future Implications and Directions

The playing field of purchasing and supply management has changed dramatically in the past 20 years or so, and the changes have accelerated rapidly in the late 1990s. Purchasing has evolved from a function that was looked to primarily for price reduction, to one that was looked to for cost reduction, to one that is now looked to for value enhancement throughout the supply chain.

The purchasing and supply manager is an important member of the business team. Purchasing managers must be good all-around business people. They must be familiar with the organization's objectives, as well as the specific objectives for each purchase. Without this knowledge, purchasing's behavior will not be in alignment with organizational goals.

Purchasing is a support function and a facilitating function. As such, it is responsible for understanding and supporting the goals of the groups that it serves. Of course, that does not mean to blindly serve; an effective purchasing manager enhances the value of the organization by:

- Understanding the needs of stakeholders
- Looking for alternatives to better meet those needs
- Challenging others when their requests do not appear to be in alignment with broader organizational goals
- Translating the objectives and results of purchasing activities into a language the stakeholders understand, in alignment with the stakeholders' objectives
- Understanding the changing marketplace and sharing knowledge with management
- Looking for revenue enhancement opportunities

As an increasing number of organizations move to a model in which purchasing must "persuade" others to use its services, purchasing has also become a sales function.[7] Increasingly, purchasing is being viewed as a revenue-enhancing function. While this activity is still in its infancy, a recent A.T. Kearney study indicates that this push will accelerate dramatically throughout the decade of the 2000s.[8]

General Motors recently announced that it will create an online marketplace for suppliers, called the GM Market Site. This Web site will allow GM's suppliers and other supply chain members to take advantage of GM's global purchasing power to reduce their costs. In turn, GM will earn transaction fees, commissions, or financing fees on all activities.[9] This is just one example of how purchasing can make a contribution as a revenue-enhancing function.

The future has great promise for proactive, progressive business people in purchasing and supply management. As organizations increasingly compete supply chain to supply chain, there will be opportunities for PSM to take on a greater role. The potential contribution of PSM is limited only by the imagination.

Key Points

1. Purchasing and supply management personnel are responsible for staying up-to-date concerning changes in supply market conditions in order to effectively perform their jobs.
2. Awareness of technological trends and availability is critical as an organization develops products or services.
3. Numerous internal and external data sources are available to help suppliers stay in touch with the market, especially since the explosion of the Internet and intranets.
4. Purchasers have numerous buying strategies available to them. The suitability of the various strategies depends on organizational forecasts and supply market trends.
5. Many types of contractual arrangements, from a single "spot buy" to a life-of-product agreement, are used today, depending on the organization's goals.
6. Decision tree analysis is a tool to help analyze the expected value of a decision.
7. Supply chain management is a holistic philosophy that considers all of the members of the supply chain, from the earliest supplier to the ultimate customer, as the unit of analysis. This broad approach is having a major impact on the way that organizations compete.
8. The future of purchasing and supply management looks positive. The expectations placed on purchasing managers will continue to grow, expanding the notion of value enhancement to include revenue enhancement.

Questions for Review

1. Why is it critical for purchasing managers to stay in touch with market trends and conditions?
2. What are some techniques for monitoring market trends and conditions?
3. What are some of the advantages and disadvantages of JIT purchasing? Under what circumstances is JIT appropriate?
4. What are commodities, and how are they bought and sold?
5. Explain the concept of consignment inventory and when it applies to an organization.
6. What is the process for developing a decision tree, and when is it appropriate?
7. What are some of the major ways that purchasing can enhance the value of an organization?
8. What is meant by purchasing revenue enhancement?

For Additional Information

Laseter, T.M. *Balanced Sourcing: Cooperation and Competition in Supplier Relationships*, Jossey-Bass, San Francisco, CA, 1998.

Monczka, R., R. Trent, and R.B. Handfield. *Purchasing and Supply Chain Management*, South-Western College Publishing, Cincinnati, OH, 1998.

NAPM InfoEdge. "Understanding Supply Chain Management," (3: 7), March 1998, pp. 1-16.

Endnotes

1. Ellram, L.M. *The Role of Supply Management in Target Costing*, Center for Advanced Purchasing Studies, Tempe, AZ, 1999.
2. Ellram, 1999.
3. Ellram, L.M. and A. Maltz. *Outsourcing: Implications for Supply Management*, Center for Advanced Purchasing Studies, Tempe, AZ, 1996.
4. Ellram and Maltz, 1996.
5. Fine, C. *Clockspeed*, Perseus Books, Reading, MA, 1998.

6. Ellram and Maltz, 1996.
7. Murphree, J. "Building a Customer-Centered Supply Chain," *Purchasing Today®*, June 1999, pp. 34-42.
8. A.T. Kearney. *Global Supply Management Trends*, A.T. Kearney, 1999.
9. *The Wall Street Journal*. "Ford and GM to Put Supply Operations Online in Rival E-Commerce Venture," November 3, 1999, p. A4.

AUTHOR INDEX

SUBJECT INDEX

Membership Application

Institute for Supply Management™, Inc.

Members are encouraged to join a local affiliated association. To obtain information on the affiliated association closest to you and dues information, please call ISM Customer Service at 800/888-6276 or 480/752-6276, extension 401. Applications can also be submitted via the Internet at www.ism.ws.

Please check the appropriate box:

❑ New Member ❑ Past Member Member ID Number (if known) _____

❑ I am replacing the following current member in my organization (If replacing a current member, send completed application to the affiliate.)

Member Name _____ ISM ID# _____

Dr. Mr. Mrs. Ms. Miss _____ _____ _____
(please circle) First Name MI Last Name

_____ _____
Title (required) Organization (required)

Please check the preferred mailing address:

❑ BUSINESS ❑ HOME

_____ _____

_____ _____

_____ _____
City State ZIP Code City State ZIP Code

_____ _____
Country Postal Code Country Postal Code

_____ _____
E-Mail E-Mail

( ) _____ ( ) _____ ( ) _____
Business Phone Number** Fax Number** Home Phone Number **

**For international numbers, please include country and city codes.

Date of Birth (optional): ___/___/___

Industry Code (choose a 3-digit code from the list provided on page two of this application): ____ ____ ____

Number of employees at your location (please check one): ❑ under 100 ❑ 100-249 ❑ 250-499 ❑ 500-999 ❑ 1000+

Education (check highest level completed): ❑ High School ❑ Associate's ❑ Bachelor's ❑ Master's ❑ Other_____
❑ Student (estimated graduation date): _____

Are you a C.P.M.? ❑ Yes ❑ No Are you an A.P.P.? ❑ Yes ❑ No

Do you hold other professional designations? If so, please list:_____

Would you like to serve on a committee? ❑ Yes ❑ No

Are you involved in sales? If so, explain: _____

MEMBERSHIP TYPE: Please select one of the options below. See back for option details.

Option I	Option II
❑ **Regular Membership** – Includes National and local affiliate benefits. I choose to become a member through (please provide affiliate name): For dues information and District/Affiliate code, contact ISM Customer Service at 800/888-6276 or 480/752-6276, extension 401. District/Affiliate Code (Code provided by ISM): ___ ___ / ___ ___ ___ Annual ISM/Affiliate Dues: USD $ _____ Administrative Fee: USD $ 20.00 Affiliate Initiation Fee: USD $ _____ Other: USD $ _____ TOTAL: USD $ _____	❑ **Direct National Membership** – Includes National benefits only. Does not include affiliate benefits. Contact ISM for dues. ISM Dues: USD $ _____ Administrative Fee: USD $ _____ TOTAL: USD $ _____ **Method of payment (U.S. Funds Only):** ❑ Personal Check ❑ Organization Check ❑ VISA ❑ MasterCard ❑ American Express ❑ Diners Club Charge Card# _____ Exp. Date ___/___ Amount to be Charged $ _____ Cardholder Signature _____

ISM members receive *Inside Supply Management*™ magazine as a $12 portion of the national membership fee. I agree to abide by the *ISM Bylaws, Principles and Standards of Ethical Supply Management Conduct*, and *Statement of Antitrust Policy*, as stated on the back of this application. A copy of the *ISM Bylaws* may be obtained by writing or calling ISM Customer Service at the address and telephone number listed below.

_____ _____
Signature Date

RETURN TO:	APPROVALS FOR AFFILIATE/ISM USE ONLY	
	ISM _____ Date _____ Affiliate _____ Date _____ Other _____ Date _____	**51** **SMKS3**

ISM Use Only

Amount $_____ Approval #_____ Date Entered _____ Initials _____

ISM, P.O. Box 22160, Tempe, AZ 85285-2160 • 800/888-6276 or 480/752-6276, extension 401 • Fax 480/752-2299

STANDARD INDUSTRY CODES (SIC) — If you have responsibility for more than one industry, please use only the one three-digit code representing the major activity of the company, division, or plant for which you work. (Write the three-digit code on the reverse side of this form in the appropriate space.)

AGRICULTURE, FORESTRY, AND FISHERIES
- 010 Agricultural production - crops
- 020 Agricultural production - livestock
- 070 Agricultural services
- 080 Forestry
- 090 Fishing, hunting, trapping

MINING
- 100 Metal mining
- 120 Bituminous coal/lignite mining
- 130 Oil and gas extraction
- 140 Nonmetallic minerals, except fuels

CONTRACT CONSTRUCTION
- 150 General building contractors
- 160 Heavy construction contractors
- 170 Special trade contractors

MANUFACTURING
- 200 Food and kindred products
- 210 Tobacco manufacturers
- 220 Textile mill products
- 230 Apparel/other textile products
- 240 Lumber and wood products
- 250 Furniture and fixtures
- 260 Paper and allied products
- 270 Printing and publishing
- 280 Chemicals and allied products
- 290 Petroleum and coal products
- 300 Rubber and miscellaneous plastic products
- 310 Leather and leather products
- 320 Stone, clay, and glass products
- 330 Primary metal industries
- 340 Fabricated metal products
- 350 Machinery, except electrical

- 360 Electric/electronic equipment
- 370 Transportation equipment
- 380 Instruments and related products
- 390 Miscellaneous manufacturing industries

TRANSPORTATION, COMMUNICATION, AND UTILITY SERVICES
- 400 Railroad transportation
- 410 Local/interurban mass transit
- 420 Trucking and warehousing
- 430 U.S. Postal Service
- 440 Water transportation
- 450 Transportation by air
- 460 Pipelines, except natural gas
- 470 Transportation services
- 480 Communication
- 490 Electric, gas, and sanitary services

WHOLESALE AND RETAIL TRADE
- 500 Wholesale trade - durable goods
- 510 Wholesale trade - nondurable goods
- 520 Building materials/garden supplies
- 530 General merchandise stores
- 540 Food stores
- 550 Automotive dealers/service stations
- 560 Apparel and accessory stores
- 570 Furniture/home furnishings stores
- 580 Eating and drinking places
- 590 Miscellaneous retail

FINANCE, INSURANCE, AND REAL ESTATE
- 600 Banking
- 610 Credit agencies, except banks
- 620 Security & commodity brokers/services
- 630 Insurance carriers

- 640 Insurance agents, brokers/services
- 650 Real estate
- 670 Holding/other investment offices

SERVICES
- 700 Hotel/other lodging places
- 720 Personal services
- 730 Business services
- 750 Auto repair, services/garages
- 760 Miscellaneous repair services
- 780 Motion pictures
- 790 Amusement/recreation services
- 800 Health services
- 810 Legal services
- 820 Educational services
- 830 Social services
- 840 Museums/botanical, zoological gardens
- 860 Membership organizations
- 870 Engineering/accounting/related services
- 880 Private households
- 890 Miscellaneous services

GOVERNMENT
- 910 Executive, legislative/general
- 920 Justice, public order, and safety
- 930 Finance, taxation, and monetary policy
- 940 Administration of human resources
- 950 Environmental quality/housing
- 960 Administration of economic programs
- 970 National security/international affairs

NONCLASSIFIABLE
- 999 Nonclassifiable establishments